HIGHER ANSWERS
FOR
Truth Seekers

Also by Sirshree

Spiritual Masterpieces: Self-realization books for serious seekers

The Secret of Awakening
100% Karma: Learn the Art of Conscious Karma that Liberates
100% Meditation: Dip into the Stillness of Pure Awareness
100% Devotion: ...Where the Devotee Disappears and Only God Remains
You are Meditation: Discover Peace and Bliss Within
Essence of Devotion: From Devotee to Divinity
Secrets of Shiva
The Supreme Quest: Your search for the truth ends there where you are
The Greatest Freedom: Discover the key to an Awakened Living
Secret of The Third Side of The Coin: Unraveling missing links in spirituality
Seek Forgiveness & be Free: Liberation from Karmic Bondage
Passwords to a Happy Life: The Art of Being Happy in All Situations

Self Help Treasures: Self-development books for success seekers

The Source of Health: The Key to Perfect Health Discovery
Inner Ninety Hidden Infinity: How to build your book of values
Inner 90 for Youth: The secret of reaching and staying at the peak of success
The Source for Youth: You have the power to change your life
Inner Magic: The Power of self-talk
The Power of Present: Experience the Joy of the Now
You are Not Lazy: A story of shifting from Laziness to Success
Freedom From Fear, Worry, Anger: How to be cool, calm and courageous
The Little Gita of Problem Solving: Gift of 18 Solutions to Any Problem
Discover Your Real Wealth: If Money is the Means, Then What is the End?

New Age Nuggets: Practical books on applied spirituality and self-help

The Source: Power of Happy Thoughts
Secret of Happiness: Instant Happiness - Here and Now!
Help God to Help You: Whatever you do, do it with a smile
Ultimate Purpose of Success: Achieving Success in all five aspects of life
Celebrating Relationships: Bringing Love, Life, Laughter in Your Relations
Everything is a Game of Beliefs: Understanding is the Whole Thing
Detachment From Attachment: Gift of Freedom From Suffering
Emotional Freedom Through Spiritual Wisdom
What To Do When the Mind Troubles You: Encountering the Mind instead of Escaping it

Profound Parables: Fiction books containing profound truths

Beyond Life: Conversations on Life After Death
The One Above: What if God was your neighbour?
The Warrior's Mirror: The Path To Peace
Master of Siddhartha: Revealing the Truth of Life and Afterlife
Put Stress to Rest: Utilizing Stress to Make Progress
The Source @ Work: A Story of Inspiration from Geeodee

HIGHER ANSWERS
FOR
Truth Seekers

ANSWERS THAT PAVE YOUR WAY
TO THE SUPREME TRUTH

SIRSHREE
Author of the bestseller *The Source*

Higher Answers for Truth Seekers

By **Sirshree** Tejparkhi

Copyright © Tejgyan Global Foundation
All Rights Reserved 2020.

Tejgyan Global Foundation is a charitable organization
with its headquarters in Pune, India.

ISBN : 978-93-90132-04-1

Published by WOW Publishings Pvt. Ltd., India.

First Edition published in July 2020.

Printed and bound by Trinity Academy for Corporate Training Ltd., Pune, India.

Based on the Hindi book *Sat-Chit-Anand* by Sirshree

Copyrights are reserved with Tejgyan Global Foundation and publishing rights are vested exclusively with WOW Publishings Pvt. Ltd. This book is sold subject to the condition that it shall not by way of trade or otherwise, be lent, resold, hired out, or otherwise circulated without the publisher's prior written consent in any form of binding or cover other than that in which it is published and without a similar condition including this condition being imposed on the subsequent purchaser and without limiting the rights under copyright reserved above, no part of this publication may be reproduced, stored in or introduced into a retrieval system, or transmitted, in any form, or by any means, electronic, mechanical, photocopying, recording or otherwise, without the prior written permission of both the copyright owner and the above-mentioned publisher of this book. Any person who does any unauthorized act in relation to this publication may be liable to criminal prosecution and civil claims for damages.

Although the author and publisher have made every effort to ensure accuracy of content in this book, they hereby disclaim any liability to any party for any loss, damage, or disruption caused by errors or omissions, resulting from negligence, accident, or any other cause. Readers are advised to take full responsibility to exercise discretion in understanding and applying the content of this book.

*This book is dedicated to seekers
who wish to attain the supreme truth
in this very life.*

Contents

Preface		11
Editor's Note		15
Section I: Eligibility for Wisdom and Surrendering		17
1.	First Condition for Self-realization	19
2.	How and Who Attains Knowledge of Truth	21
3.	Combination of Worthiness and Surrender	23
4.	Questions of the Mind	26
5.	Thirst for Truth	28
6.	Necessity of A Living Guru	31
7.	The Call for Awakening of Self	33
8.	Knowledge Can Also Be Attained in the Afterlife	35
9.	Experience of Self in the Afterlife	37
10.	Every Kind of Knowledge Has its Advantage	39

Section II: The Real Truth And Practical Spirituality — 41

11. Entangling and Detangling of Self — 43
12. How to Get Stabilized in the Self — 45
13. Fill the Emptiness with Truth — 47
14. Choosing Truth — 49
15. Free Sample Given by Nature — 51
16. How to Look at the Experiences of Meditation — 55
17. Expressing Yourself While Being in the Self-Experience — 57
18. Chanting and Experience of Self — 59
19. Recognize Your Fundamental Error — 61
20. Importance of Discipline in Spirituality — 64
21. Demonstration of Spirituality — 67
22. Let the Mind Get Effective Answers — 71
23. Understanding Paradoxical Wisdom — 75
24. Introverts and Extroverts — 77
25. Ways to Develop the Intellect — 79

Section III: The Path to Freedom — 83

26. The Path of Freedom from Negative Emotions — 85
27. Surrendering the Ego through Unconditional Devotion — 88
28. Freedom from Negative Tendencies and Patterns — 91
29. Thirst for Freedom and Spiritual Strength — 93
30. Freedom from Fear — 95

Section IV: Meditating to Attain
The Right Understanding of Meditation   97

31. Meditate with the Right Understanding   99

32. Awareness of the Body   102

33. Quality is More Important than Quantity of Meditation   105

34. Clarity of Meditation   108

35. Experience of Self in Every Moment   110

36. The Art of Living in this Illusory World   112

37. Definite Remedy for Freedom from Thoughts   114

38. Seer, Seen, and Seeing   116

Section V: Unfolding the Mysteries of Karma   119

39. Soul of Karma   121

40. Karma and Fruits of Past Lives   123

41. Karma Associated with Illness   126

42. How to Attain Liberation from Bondage of Karma   131

43. Good Karma, Bad Karma, and Akarma   134

44. The Fruit of Bad Karma   137

45. Freedom from Past Karma   139

Section VI: God, Grace, and Prayer   141

46. Is God Energy or Vibration?   143

47. Truth, Soul, and Supreme Soul   145

48. Every Prayer Has a Role   146

49. Experience Constant Grace	148
50. The Necessity of Slow People	150
51. Everything Has Already Happened	152
52. Freedom from Old Memories	155
53. Old Memories and the Next Birth	157
54. Rebirth of the Astral Body	159

Section VII: Living According To The Divine Plan — 161

55. All Possibilities Are Pre-decided	163
56. The Journey from Feelings to Action	165
57. The Divine Plan	168
58. Conviction of Truth and Limitless Thinking	170
59. The Self-expression that Benefits Everyone	172
60. Living an Impersonal Life	174
About the Author	178

Preface

If you are a truth seeker, there may be some questions and doubts popping up every now and then in your mind, such as:

Why have these specific events occurred in my life?

Who attains the truth? And how?

What exactly does 'thirst for truth' mean?

What is the first condition to attain the truth?

How can we become worthy of attaining the truth and how can we surrender to the truth?

While treading the path of spirituality, how can we deal with various hurdles such as negative emotions, thoughts, tendencies, various fears, and ego?

What is the actual basis of the fruit of karma and how can we attain freedom from bondage of karma?

How can meditation help us to attain Self-realization and to get established in the Self?

How can we develop complete conviction on the truth? How can we shift from knowledge of truth to experience of truth?

What if we cannot attain the truth in this life? Is it possible in the afterlife?

What is the Divine Plan?

If any of the above questions and more have been churning within you, and you have been seeking the deeper answers, not just superficial ones, then you have arrived at the right place.

You may or may not have found the answers to some of your questions in spite of trying, while some answers may have been difficult to understand. During the challenging times of your life, many questions would have arisen in your mind. If you don't get the right answers, you may get stuck in the web of those questions. Some questions are asked only for gaining information and some for self-development. On the other hand, there are some questions that are capable of transforming your perspective and your way of life. This is the kind of questions that this book deals with.

The answers are such that they can take you to another level and enable you to see the big picture. They can bring about a paradigm shift in your understanding of yourself, of life and its various aspects, and the world at large.

If you have embarked on the quest of truth and have been treading the path since some time, then you may be already aware of some higher truths, such as: Only the Self exists (which you may call as God, the Almighty, the Creator, Paramatma, Allah, Holy spirit, Consciousness, the truth, the supreme truth, a higher power, or any other name). The Self is limitless, formless, omnipresent, omnipotent, and possesses every known and unknown attribute. It is 'nothing' with the potential of everything. Only the Self is the truth. Everything else is an illusion (*maya*) created by the Self.

Why create anything in the first place, one may ask. Well, there is nothing and no one else besides the Self; that's why it needs something to experience and express itself. Hence, it created from itself all these universes and everything inside them. It also created certain rules to operate these universes, which we call as universal laws or laws of nature. Every game needs some rules, right? This is all part of the elaborate divine game or *leela*.

But, why is it an illusion? Because it's the Self which is operating through everything and every body, although it appears as if they are operating on their own.

The most important thing to understand and remember is that absolutely everything—living as well as non-living—is the Self. You are not the body or the mind; you are the Self. You have forgotten this, but this too is part of the game. Your ultimate purpose on Earth is to know your true self (Self-realization), get permanently established in the Self (Self-stabilization), and to express the divine qualities of the Self (Self-expression).

This is the premise on which the answers have been given to various questions of truth seekers. So, let's dive in and gather the radiant pearls of wisdom. They will help you in overcoming obstacles and to progress on the path to become who you truly are—the limitless, boundless, ever-blissful Self.

Editor's Note

This book is a compilation of profound answers to questions put forth by truth seekers. It is important to mention here that Sirshree's answers to a seeker's questions depend on the seeker's spiritual maturity and ability to grasp the subtleness of the topic. The answers also change according to the background and context of the seeker. Hence, the same question can have different answers at different times.

This book provides answers for seekers who have attained some level of spiritual maturity and are intended to help them attain further clarity in order to progress to higher levels in their spiritual journey.

Seekers receive and experience the highest answers as they grow in their spiritual practice. This is the beauty of Sirshree's *System for Wisdom*, which is followed in Tej Gyan Foundation. You receive wisdom step by step and progress systematically on the path of truth. As you apply the teachings to your everyday life and see the results, you develop conviction on the teachings. This conviction makes you receptive to a higher level of knowledge and practices, which you again start applying. In this way, you continue to advance till you reach the ultimate goal.

While reading this book, another important point to note is that some answers may tally with scriptures or religious texts that you may have read, because the supreme truth is one and the same. On the other hand, some answers may be different from what you may have heard or read, because some aspects of the truth cannot be expressed in words and yet every self-realized soul tries to express it in their own way, for the benefit of seekers who are listening to them.

This book covers a variety of questions, and hence some intricate topics cannot be covered in their entirety in this book. If you wish to gain complete knowledge on those topics, books by Sirshree on those specific topics are also available, which have been indicated in footnotes in this book.

All the answers that have appeared in this book are such that they can bring about a radical shift in your understanding. Some answers may amaze you and some may give you an "*aha*" moment. So, let's begin this blessed journey to receive and imbibe the higher answers, which will pave your way to the supreme truth.

SECTION I

Eligibility for Wisdom and Surrendering

1
First Condition For Self-realization

Sometimes I feel that those who have a leisurely lifestyle can attain Self-realization sooner than those who lead a fast-paced life. Is this notion correct? those who lead a fast-paced life. Is this notion correct?

To begin with, please understand that there is no need to fix a formula for Self-realization. Whether a person's lifestyle is fast-paced or leisurely has absolutely no bearing on their likelihood of attaining Self-realization sooner or later. The fact is, both hyperactive as well as indolent people have attained Self-realization. The common factor in them was, when they realized the futility of the life they were leading in this world, they developed an intense thirst and love for liberation. Thus began their journey to find the ultimate truth.

The fact is, in humans, the most basic and the most important is the experience of Self. That is what makes a difference, that is what deepens your understanding, and that is what stimulates your thirst and love for truth and liberation. Once Self-realization and stabilization in the Self is attained, anything that happens outside makes no difference to you.

When you don't know the real reason behind why a person is leading a fast-paced life, you cannot ascertain whether they have a thirst for truth or their tendencies are making them run around. The same applies to a chilled-out person.

If a person is running around in unawareness, it will definitely take them a long time to attain Self-realization. But if they are aware, it will take less time. If they are totally unaware, they won't even realize whether they are running around or lying around lazily. This is why awareness is crucial. On the other hand, if a person is lethargic but aware, then there is full possibility of Self-realization. Because due to awareness, they can see everything and be a witness to everything that is happening.

Whether you are hyperactive or lazy, you have to take help of that very attribute to attain Self-realization. But the most important prerequisite is to be aware and conscious. For those who are living unconsciously, it doesn't matter if they are hyperactive or indolent; it is going to take a long time for them to attain Self-realization. Therefore, don't make any assumptions or jump to conclusions. If everything is being done with awareness, there is a definite possibility of Self-realization. The first condition for it is to be aware.

2
How and Who Attains Knowledge of Truth

It is said that knowledge of truth can be either 100% or zero, then what is the level of my knowledge? And who gets this knowledge—the mind or the Self?

You need to understand the exact context in which it has been said that knowledge is either 100% or zero. It's about knowledge of Self or *being*. This is what we call as 'Bright knowledge' or *Tejgyan*. One may either have this knowledge or not, and that's why it is said so.

A seeker of the ultimate truth acquires knowledge in steps. They gain shifts in their understanding at every step, which helps them to realize the ultimate truth. Take a moment to reflect upon the difference in your state earlier and now. If your state today is such that you are able to understand the experience of *being*, then you have to attain and apply further spiritual practices to eliminate the tendencies of your mind and to stabilize in this experience of *being*. In this context, your state today is that of applying further spiritual practices.

In answer to your second question, it's the Self that attains knowledge as well as awareness. When you listen to discourses, it gets recorded in your brain, and is used by both the Self and the mind.

There is only one living entity in an individual, and that is the

Self. The Self receives knowledge, which creates inner shifts in its understanding, which then gets recorded in the tape-recorder of the brain. Thereafter, when the Self gets entangled in situations, it wrongly assumes itself to be an individual (the false 'I', the original ego) and makes wrong use of the knowledge. Upon awakening, it uses the knowledge for expression of its divine attributes. In this manner, the awakened Self as well as the entangled Self, which can also be called as the mind, both make use of the knowledge.

3
Combination of Worthiness and Surrender

After acquiring spiritual knowledge, how does the ego rise and how does it surrender?

Every person should be interested in getting rid of the tendency of showing off one's special qualities and becoming free of ego. In the beginning, one may not have spiritual knowledge but it is only after attaining knowledge that the real test begins. One receives something only when they have become worthy of it, but the irony is that quite often their worthiness disappears after receiving it.

Let's consider an example. If you keep a coin on water, it sinks at once. But if it is very light weight, it can float. You may have seen children trying this experiment, where they let the water calm down, then very gently place a light coin on the surface of water, and it floats. It can be said this coin has developed the capability, eligibility, or worthiness to float on water. However, if you add even a grain of rice on the surface of this coin, it will sink. This means that an individual becomes worthy of something and receives it. Thereafter, he begins to get something new, but then he has to again increase his capability and eligibility in order to retain it.

If the coin becomes egoistic after floating once, and thinks that now it can always float, then it will sink under the weight of its own ego. This error is so subtle that one doesn't even realize when the ego appears after becoming worthy. One begins to get thoughts like, "Now I know everything... I know it all... People praise me, but they have no knowledge... they haven't had that experience which I got so early on... I was sitting in meditation when this happened and that happened... most people don't get such experiences so easily..." If such thoughts arise even after receiving knowledge, then you should know these thoughts are only boosting the ego.

If a teacher thinks, "I know everything and these students know nothing," then this is ego. The only difference between the teacher and students is that the knowledge has reached the teacher and is yet to reach the students. Everything is happening spontaneously according to the laws of nature, and hence there's no need for the ego to arise. But it crops up because one has not yet tasted the joy of a pure mind.

Suppose, an individual wishes to establish his position among people by displaying his special attributes. Then, if he gets spiritual knowledge, he wouldn't want to surrender in devotion. But if he considers the ego as his enemy which should be eliminated, he will ask himself, "Who am I in reality?" On contemplating, he will understand that whatever little knowledge he has received is only because occasionally he became worthy of it for some time, otherwise he wouldn't have received it. But the ego emerges and takes credit by claiming, "All the spiritual knowledge and experience I have gained is because of my efforts."

Only after surrendering, the realization dawns that this knowledge is attained only when the individual (the false 'I', the original ego) surrenders. This realization or insight is of great help in every person's life. It's due to this insight that one loses interest in showing off one's special qualities, and is instead concerned about enhancing devotion and dissolving the ego.

You should also keep working on this insight in your life, even if some mistakes occur along the way. After all, you learn from your mistakes. Therefore, without getting scared of making errors, continue listening and reading the truth as well as reflecting honestly on it, so that your understanding always remains fresh. If you can do this, your relationships will become more loving and your ego will also surrender.

4
Questions of the Mind

What have I done to deserve this grace, due to which I am receiving the highest things in life and also the highest wisdom?

Such questions, when answered, will only inflate one's ego. Suppose, you are told that you received a particular thing because you have an attractive personality, then your ego is bound to expand. That's why it's no use getting answers to such questions. So, let the mind continue its chatter and you ask yourself, "Who is asking this question? And on whom has this divine grace been bestowed?" The essence of grace is that it is unconditional. Only a true devotee receives such grace.

The egoistic mind always seeks a logical answer—one that will make it feel exceptional. It wants to hear from the Guru, "You are unique and special." People want to hear distinctive statements like, "You were a yogi, you were highly knowledgeable and wise in your past life. That's why you are different from others in this life. You are special." Avoid listening to such things as long as your ego is susceptible to swelling. This is the phase you are currently going through.

The ego will pop up intermittently and seek credit by declaring, "All this grace has been conferred upon *me*." You have to ask the mind, "*Who* has actually been graced? Is it the ego, or is it the

Self showering grace on the Self?" Rather than getting entangled in meaningless questions of the mind, it's better to engage in deep contemplation of the wisdom you are receiving. When true wisdom dawns upon you, the mind will automatically surrender.

5
Thirst for Truth

'Thirst for truth' means thirst for exactly what? Is it a thirst for answers to the questions, which results in the feeling of freedom?

Thirst for truth means a deep desire to know, "What is the reality?" Suppose, you go someplace and see a building under construction. You find many different activities being carried out by different people. You observe that among these people, some are happy, some are getting angry, and yet others are doing something else. You are told to join in and start doing whatever they are doing. You wonder what exactly is going on, what is the reality here, when did this construction begin, who started it, who is the owner, and so forth.

You decide to meet the founder and ask some questions like, "What is all this? What are all these people doing? What is the purpose of coming here?" You want the answers, so that you can know the truth and do your job in the best way possible. If this kind of curiosity does not arise in your mind and you don't try to find the truth, it means you are leading your life in ignorance. That's why it is important to acquire the right understanding.

If you have that curiosity, you start probing the matter and asking people, "Why are you constructing this building? Why in this manner?" People reply, "We don't know; everyone before us was doing this in this manner, and that's why we are doing it too."

This is what happens in life. Most people have no clue why they have received this life and why they are leading their life in this way. If you ask them, their answer is, "This is the way our elders lived and so we are doing the same." But you may have further questions, like: "Why are you doing whatever you are doing? What is the reason? What will it result in? Even if you accomplish it till the end of your life, what will happen? What is the reality of this life? What is the truth?" If you ask them these questions, it will become clear that people have never deliberated along these lines. If they do, they will start seeking the truth. Because if there is love for truth, then they will find the truth and start living it.

Since we don't know the truth, we lament at things we should be happy about, and feel happy for things we should be lamenting about. When we have lived in this manner for quite some time, we get a strong thought: "I should know the truth, so that I can lead my life in the right way." This is thirst for truth.

If you are seeking the truth, then understand that this world is a maze created by God. We have to find the right door which can lead us out of this maze. If you find it, then no sorrow in the world can touch you, because you would know how to step out of the maze. This is love for freedom.

When you understand all of this, the secret will unfold that the door which can get you out of the maze was always walking right behind you. But nobody knows this truth.

The thirst for truth will awaken only when you have a deep love for freedom and devotion. Living in this state gives you immense joy. Because this building, or in other words, your body, is created for joy and not for misery. So, the question arises, what is it that you are unaware of? What is the truth? It is your right to know it, and that's why you shall know it. And you will do whatever it takes to become worthy for the truth, but you won't settle for anything less. This is love for truth.

When you really understand this, your love for freedom rises automatically. This is grace. When this grace is bestowed upon you, the ego within you surrenders and you begin to walk the path of truth.

6
Necessity of a Living Guru

Why is the role of a living Guru important in spirituality?

It is very important for every individual to have a living Guru in their life. Most people become receptive for truth in the presence of a living Guru. As technology is progressing, people are becoming less receptive for truth and indulging increasingly in ego-boosting gadgets. The basic honesty required for becoming a seeker is getting lost as people have learnt to get entangled, to forget, or to manipulate things in their favor. The role of a living Guru is critical because only a Guru can instruct the seeker to stop this.

If a person is highly receptive, then nature itself is the biggest guru for them, as it is teaching something all the time. They can learn everything from nature. There have been a few people in history who have learnt the supreme truth in this manner. However, most people lack such receptivity.

With time, the need is increasing for someone to guide us as soon as we make a mistake, so that we don't form any bad habit in the first place. If you happen to be graced with a living Guru in your life, it will play a crucial role in your internal and external growth. This is why a living Guru has been given so much importance.

To make a long story short, if you have a living Guru, you can find the path to the next level. In any era, neither the speaker nor the listeners have had so much time that everything can be revealed in one go. Most importantly, seekers don't have the receptivity for that. Therefore, the main task of every individual is to work on enhancing one's receptivity. If a living Guru is present in your life, your receptivity increases automatically, and even if you are not very receptive, you still get the inspiration to move ahead. Hence the need of a living Guru.

However, there are some impersonators or fake gurus, who take advantage of this fact. Anywhere in the world, wherever there are seekers who are stuck in their spiritual journey instead of progressing, it is because some fake gurus have misused this fact. This is the reason that people have moved away from the real truth.

There have been claims that the next guru will not manifest for another 500 years. Seekers are ruining their possibilities of liberation by believing in such lies. Fake gurus perpetuate such wrong beliefs and spread ignorance to fulfil their own selfish agendas. You don't have to accept any such beliefs; instead you just need to take benefit of the wisdom you have received.

Nature is always playing the role of a guru, which makes spiritual progress possible in every era and every age. Just keep working on increasing your receptivity, and take full advantage if you have a living Guru*. Remember not to believe in statements of wrong individuals. You can progress on the spiritual path at any place, at any time, and in any situation.

---

*You can read in detail on the role of a guru in Sirshree's book *Light of Grace*.

7
The Call for Awakening of Self

Does a seeker find a Guru or does the Guru call seekers towards himself when they become worthy?

An individual (the false 'I' within, the ego) always wants to hear from the Guru that they are so virtuous and have done so many good deeds, because of which the Guru has called them and they have reached here. The individual wants to take credit. But as their understanding grows, they realize whom the Guru actually calls. The Guru only calls the Self or Consciousness, and nobody else.

Your preparations and practices to progress on the path of truth awaken your inner guru—the Self. There are many things that happen in life, which you don't like and don't want to happen. This gives rise to a prayer within you for getting rid of ignorance and attaining the truth. In fact, it is this prayer which proves to be the most beneficial in your life. You are communicating exactly what you want. You are conveying that you want the path which will keep you happy at all times. This prayer attracts all positive things to you, and in case those things are not available on Earth, they begin to get created. The creative thoughts for their creation reach the minds of some people and that work is accomplished through them. This is the way things are being done all over the planet. But an individual wants to take credit for every little thing owing to ego. However, one gradually understands that only the Self exists, there is nothing else.

It's the divine game of the Self that is going on upon this Earth as well as in the life after death. When this becomes clear, one's life is filled only with joy.

This answer basically means that the Guru does not call any individual but only the Self, because it's the Self within the individual that needs to be awakened.

8
Knowledge Can Also Be Attained in the Afterlife

Do those people, who did not get a Guru in this life, receive knowledge of truth in the afterlife? How do they prepare for it?

Yes, knowledge of truth can also be attained in the afterlife.

It's important to understand that the Guru is available everywhere. The Guru is not an individual. Guru is the limitless and formless Self, and the Self is present in each and every thing. Nature too is always giving guidance and knowledge of truth, be it on Earth or in the life after death. But until someone becomes totally receptive, they cannot receive the guidance or knowledge being given by nature. For those who are *not* receptive, the process of preparing them to become receptive goes on in their earthly life and then they receive the knowledge of truth in their afterlife.

Flexibility is the most important requirement to develop receptivity. Also, it is essential to get rid of the habit of jumping to conclusions. Whenever one hears anything, there is a tendency to arrive at a conclusion and to stamp it: *This is how people are... this world is bad... God always does this... There is nobody when you need them...* and so on. They then judge everybody based on such conclusions. If they can challenge these conclusions and see new possibilities, only then do they open up to guidance. That's when they can receive the knowledge of truth.

Therefore, the question is not whether someone has a Guru or not. The Guru is available in everyone's life, but people are not able to recognize the Guru, and hence cannot receive the guidance for attaining the truth. This is why, the first task that the Guru carries out is to enhance a person's receptivity, so they can receive that guidance wherever possible—whether on Earth or in the afterlife*. Thus, whether they receive that guidance on Earth or not, they are definitely progressing by increasing their receptivity.

---

*You can read more about life after death or the afterlife in Sirshree's books *Beyond Life* and *Master of Siddhartha*.

9
Experience of Self in the Afterlife

If I cannot experience the Self in this life on Earth, can it happen in the afterlife, or will I have to take a body again?

When it is possible to experience the Self in this earthly life, then it is also possible in the afterlife. That's why the question is flawed when it states, "*If* I cannot experience the Self in this life…" When you have not clearly understood the guidance that you have been given, only then does the question of 'if' arise. Hence, first think over what is hampering you, because of which this 'if' has arisen, this doubt has arisen in your mind.

The tendency of thinking, "If this happens… if that happens…" will follow you in your afterlife too. All arrangements have been made on Earth to experience the Self, but if tendencies of the mind are working so strongly here, they will become even more powerful in the afterlife. In spite of that, guidance will be provided to you even there. The possibility of experiencing the Self is available in both realms, but the mind wants to be lazy and thinks, "If the Self can be experienced in the afterlife as well, then what's the rush to experience it here?"

Those who have this attitude will not experience it in the afterlife too. The Self can be experienced with the astral body also, but if you cannot do it with the physical body, then it is difficult with the astral body as well. Let us understand this with the help of an analogy.

Suppose, you are trying to listen to the radio, but there is so much noise outside that you have to put your ear close to the radio. Yet you are making the effort to listen. If in such a situation, the radio's volume goes even lower, then how can you hear it? You will have to make even more effort to listen to the subtle sound; you will have to train your ears even further.

Similarly, if it's difficult for you to experience the Self with your physical body due to distractions, then it would be even more challenging with your astral body since it is very subtle in nature.

The only solution is to eliminate your tendencies on Earth itself. Examine and find out the areas in which your mind makes excuses with "if…" and continues to procrastinate. When you have done this, you will become open to possibilities on Earth.

10
Every Kind of Knowledge Has its Advantage

Earlier I used to attend a *satsang* where the Guru used to make us meditate on the breath. Now when I try to apply the new knowledge and practices that I have received here, my attention keeps going to the breath. Is this okay?

To begin with, please understand that there is nothing right or wrong with that. You only need to decide whether you want to benefit from the new knowledge you are receiving or you want to work only on the breath.

Suppose, it's time for a student to study, but instead he begins to exercise. There is no harm in exercising; in fact, it is highly beneficial. But now, he has to decide whether he wants to benefit from studying as well. If yes, then he will study at the right time and exercise at the right time.

The point being made is that you will have to develop the discipline within you to benefit from the new knowledge being given to you.

You have worked on the breath and also gained from it. Now that you are getting new knowledge, do ask yourself, "Do I want this or not?" Because both are not contradictory to each other. Everything is good in itself. Exercise, diet, as well as the knowledge of truth—everything has its own significance. Everything should be allocated its right place. Shoes are to be worn on the feet and glasses are to be worn over the eyes. If you interchange them, there will be a problem.

Take advantage of both, the old and the new. To do so, it would be best to allot specific time slots for each activity. Just as we have fixed the time for World Peace Prayer for global healing at 9:09 in the morning and at night, so that it is easy for everyone to tune in and pray together. Likewise, create different time slots for the new spiritual practice and for working on the breath.

No effort goes in vain. Just keep in mind that you should always continue to progress and never get stuck anywhere.

You are doing good with whatever you are doing today. Every spiritual knowledge that is available in the universe has some role in helping you to grow. You have to take advantage of it and keep moving ahead. Otherwise, most people get stuck at certain points and think, "Maybe I should stop this practice because I need to work on that other practice." This often happens with those who are engaged in spiritual practices related to the physical body. For example, if someone gives them a specific word for chanting a million times, they will begin at once. However, what's the use even if this goal of chanting is completed, if they don't understand *who* is chanting and why? This is the reason people become egoistic even after becoming *sattvik** and attaining spiritual powers. They haven't understood the supreme truth. It is essential to know and experience the truth, and then to abide in it.

May this answer inspire you to be receptive to new knowledge. It's progressive to be always open to learning new things. Always choose the new and do everything with understanding.

---

*Sattvik: Balanced, equanimous, and virtuous.

SECTION II

The Real Truth
And
Practical Spirituality

11
Entangling and Detangling of Self

Why does the Self get entangled with an individual body and later detangle itself?

Suppose, you are given two choices and you have to choose one.

The first is that you are whole and complete since you are the Self, you will always remain whole and complete, and not create this world.

The second is that you will create this world and forget your true self, but there is 1% chance of remembering and returning onto yourself.

In the first scenario, there won't be a world but you will remain for eternities. However, you will never be able to know yourself or experience your presence, since there is nothing else present. You won't be aware of your existence, since nothing else exists to see, hear, touch, taste, or feel.

In the second scenario, you create the world and then have 1% possibility of knowing yourself through a human body. You will be able to experience yourself… you can realize your formless state and express it in words… you can venerate and glorify it… you can enjoy that state… you can fully understand what you really are…

by becoming so many different people, you can share the joy with others and express yourself in different ways.

So, which of the two scenarios would you choose? Because this will make it clear why the Self created the world and why it entangles and detangles itself.

Obviously, you would choose the second option.

When the Self creates this world, there is a high possibility of getting entangled with the human body and forgetting itself, but there is also 1% possibility of detanglement and realizing itself. This is the reason the Self chooses the second option. Those people, who have been graced with a Guru, have a lesser possibility of getting entangled and forgetting the Self.

Had the Self not created the world, it would have never been able to express itself. It remained in the original state of nothingness for millions of years, and only then was the world created. Initially the astral dimension came into existence and later on the Earth. Scientists find this strange and unbelievable.

Gradually, as science catches up with this knowledge and a mobile phone is invented which connects Earth to the astral dimension, then it will become easy for science to understand everything. Then everyone will be able to speak with their relatives who have passed away and all the mysteries will be solved. Otherwise, people keep thinking about how this world was created, what is a black hole, what lies in deep space, what lies beyond, and so on. Until science comprehends all of this in scientific language, people will not believe this.

If this is to be explained in spiritual terms, it will be said that you don't like the state of the first scenario even now. This world has come into existence after remaining in that initial state for eons. This is the only way the truth can be expressed in words.

12
How to Get Stabilized in the Self

Does one have to go through a lengthy process to get stabilized in the Self? Or is it possible to get stabilized all of sudden in a 'eureka moment'?

Getting stabilized in the Self means getting permanently established in the Self. It means you always abide in the Self and operate as the unlimited Self that you are, and not as a limited individual that you thought you were.

There is no fixed process for stabilization in the Self. Both the possibilities that you mentioned exist. But a step by step process is more convenient for most people and hence this method has become better known. In this process, a person regularly listens to discourses on truth, then devotion arises, and the ego surrenders completely. In this way, one receives knowledge of truth and gets stabilized in the Self. However, there are many other possible ways too.

Consider Ramana Maharishi's life. At the age of 16, Self-realization and stabilization occurred all of a sudden and his body-mind were stunned into silence. He was so absorbed in the experience of the Self that he remained silent for many years. He then gradually emerged from the silence and expressed the truth in the most beautiful manner, which has benefitted so many seekers till date. The sudden stabilization in the Self can be called as a 'eureka effect.'

It can be compared to an airplane having a sudden crash landing. Hence, this process of stabilization can cause some other effects too. But the Self has experimented in different ways with different kinds of body-minds.

There are many types of body-minds, which have been guided to stabilization through varying methods by the Self. It is observed that, most of the times, knowledge of truth is given in an organized, step by step manner, as it is more suitable for most people. That's why this method has gained prominence.

In the case of a sudden landing or eureka effect, the person may have to face various difficulties. Seeing this, others may get disturbed. When people see a sudden and massive change in an individual, they get scared of spirituality. That person's seemingly 'illogical' statements and 'weird' behavior could discourage people who are interested in spirituality and cause them to back off.

This is why the eureka effect process is not publicized much and its features or details are not discussed a lot. Otherwise, people may start avoiding spirituality. And that which should be an inspiring event may become the cause of demotivation. Therefore, it is best to proceed step by step. If there is love for liberation and thirst for truth, then this is not a lengthy process. In fact, with this process, one attains the right understanding and progresses smoothly on the path of truth.

13

Fill the Emptiness with Truth

Although everything is going well in life, why do we sometimes feel emptiness? How can we use it to attain the truth?

When people feel emptiness, they begin to reflect and rethink on their life. As a result, they start doing something new and stop some old activities which they feel are not helping them. Thereby, they progress in their journey.

If you look back at your past, you will realize that whenever such a phase occurred, you always grew from that experience. Thus, whenever depression or emptiness appears, it always leads to growth, but we forget this. In fact, the feeling of emptiness is an indication that you have yet to learn some things and yet to reach some depths. It is part of nature's process.

When you are feeling empty, it is important not to stop working on whatever you have been working. Continue it with patience and perseverance. In the beginning, one tries to fill up the emptiness with material things, but soon realizes that it doesn't help. Emptiness is so vast that only the biggest thing in the world can fill it: the truth. Until it is filled with truth, this emptiness will persist. Hence, you have to consider that it is an intrinsic part of your inner growth process and its intermittent occurrence is in fact auspicious.

Whenever emptiness is labeled as something wrong, that's when confusion begins. You feel that emptiness should never occur. However, it is one of the signals that the Self gives, which needs to be contemplated in writing. When you do that, you will get an insight about which aspects of your life are lacking and need to be worked upon. Take a look at your body to see what is it lacking, how much self-confidence have you gained, and so forth. When you will ponder along such lines, the emptiness will slowly become a medium for your growth.

You have to make it a blessing and not a curse. Otherwise, people feel distressed by emptiness and turn towards wrong outlets. Since you have already found the right path, then without labelling it as something bad, employ the emptiness for progressing ahead.

14

Choosing Truth

When we are working on the path of truth, there are people who discourage us and even create obstacles. At such times, what understanding should we have?

Walking on the path of truth requires courage. You can remind yourself, "How long will people turn their face from the truth?" People can at the most postpone for some time that which is bound to happen in the future, but they cannot stop it. When the sun is rising, the mountains or the clouds can hide it only for so long; eventually the sun will shine. Till then, it is essential to have patience. In due course, you realize that the thirst for truth and expression of truth cannot be prevented for long, because everyone's ultimate desire is the same. Our core nature is the same and so we all yearn for the same thing, which is the supreme truth or supreme bliss, because this is what resides within each one of us.

Through the ages, the truth has been explained in various terms so as to make it easier for people to understand. On the other hand, this often gives rise to misunderstandings and people feel all those different words mean different things, and that it is not meant for them. This is the problem with words. Every knowledge needs to be imparted in some words, and its reminders will also be given in some words. But when people hear those words, they say, "This belongs to that language, that religion, that caste, that country…" The mind will stick some label or the other. But gradually, it becomes clear to people that all those different words mean the same—the truth is one and the same. Thereafter, they begin to like it and cooperate with you.

When you choose the path of truth, you may find that people tease you, or create obstacles in your way, or try to lead you astray with the help of *maya*. In spite of all this, you have to continue to abide by your guru's instructions. Even if no one helps you on the path, you know the value of the experience of Self that you have tasted. That's why you will give importance to truth and not to what people say. The fact is that your own experience of truth is the biggest proof that you have chosen the right path. In your further journey, you may meet new people who have different opinions and behaviors, but since you have experienced life on the path of truth, you won't get entangled in their ways or opinions.

With time, you will understand that people always try to discourage you in the beginning. As time passes, those very people are going to help you on the path of truth. Convert the hurdles created by people into stepping stones to move ahead. If you take advantage of each impediment and keep marching forward, your self-confidence will definitely rise.

15
Free Sample Given by Nature

A few days ago, I had such an experience during meditation, which I cannot describe in words, but it did not last long. Why did this happen?

Having an experience which cannot be described in words is nothing but grace. But the mind wants an answer to every 'why.' It will always ask questions like: "Why did this experience occur? Then why did it disappear?" The fact is, these experiences keep occurring in many people. Even those who don't have spiritual knowledge get such experiences; it's just that they don't recognize it. You can recognize it because you have received this knowledge.

Nature keeps giving free samples of this experience to everyone. When you visit a food items exhibition, you find various items on sale, such as pickles, chutneys, etc. The vendors give you a taste of a small free sample, so that you will like it and buy it. Similarly, nature gives you free samples of the experience of Self, which you tasted a few days ago. But if you insist for an answer in words, then it can be said that many people become passionate truth seekers only after getting a taste of this free sample from nature. They then yearn for that experience once more, which spurs them towards the path of truth. Everyone loves this experience so much that they want it repeatedly.

The fact is that the experience does not disappear, it only gets covered by the curtain of ego. Due to misunderstanding, people believe that the experience is not there anymore, that they will have to make efforts to bring it back, and only then it will return. Due to such thinking, they are under the illusion that the experience is gone. Although, with time, such misunderstandings also disappear.

The fact is, people desire to have that experience again because their understanding of Self hasn't deepened to an extent that they can recognize the essence of that experience. The mind wants to have the exact same experience once more. That's why one gets stuck in this desire, because the mind that wants to duplicate everything is always present. This is what makes the process even more difficult. When you first had that experience, you were free of any desires or expectations, and so the experience was clear. But later that desire arose.

During certain incidents, some people are able to see themselves separate from their body. During some road accidents, people describe, "After falling from the vehicle, I was standing there, while my body was lying on the road." Some people get this experience when they are deeply absorbed in work and some during meditation. You may have had it in any way, but what you have to understand is that it is available even now, but the mind wants it in the exact same way as before. Hence, you feel you are not able to experience it again.

What you need to do now is to let go and practice meditation without any expectations or conditions. There should be no stipulation for the same experience to recur. It is fine even if it never occurs again. When you don't put any conditions, every path becomes easy and all possibilities open up. As soon as stipulations enter the picture, the duplicator, i.e. the mind, comes in and creates obstacles. That's why it's best to continue practicing meditation unconditionally. When you gain understanding, you will realize that thoughts have stopped during *samadhi*, but even when thoughts are present, it's important to be able to perceive the detached experience which you get in samadhi. After all, we have to live in this world. Thus, even while living in this world, even while seeing all the scenes and situations, even in the presence of thoughts, you have to be present with the Self.

The irony is that even if you get the same experience again, the mind will immediately pop up and say, "I had this experience, and I want it once more." And you will again start making efforts for the same. This cycle will go on and on. The mind will always desire to remain in that state, because outside there are problems, pains, and sufferings.

Once a question had been asked to seekers here, that if you could instantly reach samadhi with the click of a button present on your forehead, what would happen? If this were really possible and everyone had this on-off switch, how would the world be functioning? On hearing this, everyone felt happy and said it would be simply great if this became possible. But the question is, if this were actually the case, would we have progressed? Because then everyone would just be sitting around with their buttons switched on. It would be like drug addicts who get stoned and are found lying around here and there. People would switch on the button as soon as they felt even a little unhappy. This is why samadhi is not supposed to be that easy. If someone is to be given this button, they will first have to develop eligibility for it.

You have to practice meditation rigorously to reach the state of samadhi; and this practice itself makes you capable for it. This is because when you do attain that state, you should be able to handle it properly and also make proper use of it. It should not happen that once someone tastes samadhi, they do nothing else but try to taste it again. Therefore, it is essential to make them capable of handling this state. If the Self wanted, this button would have been inbuilt in every human being. But this was not done, since otherwise people wouldn't do anything else and there would be no internal growth. Even a little stress would have made them push the button, so that awareness of the body-mind would disappear, and they would forget everything that caused the stress. People use drugs and alcohol because they want to experience extraordinary states again and again. That is why, they go on increasing the dosage.

Consider the good experience that you had in meditation as grace and know that it is available to you even when thoughts are going on. There is no need to have the same experience as the last one which you liked so much. If it recurs, it's a bonus, but if it doesn't, that shouldn't affect your understanding. Because, most important is the understanding that is gained through that experience. When there is total faith in the Guru's teachings, the seeker accepts the teachings, starts living accordingly, and gradually realizes everything. But when there is lack of faith, then seekers are required to work deeply, so that they can experience the same truth within themselves and then develop the conviction.

Be grateful for the free sample given by nature and continue your practice of meditation unconditionally.

16
How to Look at the Experiences of Meditation

Immediately after a meditation session, sometimes I can recall that during meditation there was a state in which I could clearly recognize that this is the body and I am not the body. Later on, when I try to remember that experience and everything that happened at that time, I cannot recall it. What is the reason for this?

Suppose, a king plays the role of a gardener for some time every day in his garden. He gets totally immersed in it and does not remember anything else at that time. The question is, how will the king look at this state? The fact is, it would not bother him because the king is always a king, no matter what role he plays.

But when you have an experience in meditation and cannot recall certain aspects of it, you feel, "Oh! I cannot remember things that I used to." Actually, you should be focusing on what would happen in your next session of meditation. This will motivate you to continue the practice every day. Gradually, you will start focusing more on the experience of *being* during meditation, and automatically stop getting stuck in anything else. Then it won't make a difference to you whether you remember an experience or not. Because, by then, you would have learnt how to look at every experience without any attachment.

When you reach the depths of meditation, you will experience the sense of *being* and know the answer to, "Who am I?" When you ask this question to yourself numerous times, then this question will pop up within you at the beginning of every thought and every event.

Samadhi is the final goal of meditation. Meditation will help you to progress on the path to samadhi. It will remove the beliefs present within you that are a barrier between you and samadhi. Whenever you meditate on "Who am I?", you will get a new direction. A new truth will emerge before you and all your wrong beliefs will be shaken. You will develop the conviction that you are not the body. You will become aware of your *being*. This is why you need to continue the practice of meditation without any preconceived notions.

17
Expressing Yourself While Being in the Self-experience

How can we express ourself while being in the experience of Self?

Expressing yourself while being in the experience of Self means having firm conviction of your true nature every moment and taking decisions based on that. When you have that conviction, only those decisions will arise from you that lead you towards the final destination of Self-stabilization. Gradually, all the decisions that arise from wrong tendencies and pleasure-seeking desires of the mind will go on reducing.

Be what you are in essence, consider the body as your tool, and then observe what is the highest choice that you are making in this moment. For instance, your reading this book is the highest choice you have made in this moment. It is absolutely right for this moment. The need of the next moment could be something else, which would then be the highest choice. You make different choices in different phases of your life. Where do you want to spend your time? With friends, or family, or alone—you have to make the highest choice. When you make the highest choice in every situation, in a way you are expressing your true self.

If you make choices assuming yourself to be the body, then all your decisions would be for the comfort of the body and pleasure of the senses. When the understanding seeps in that the body is merely a tool, you would want to make it sharp and efficient. To do so, you will exercise your body and mind. If the body-mind has worked the whole day, you would also provide it with rest, so that it can perform even better the next day. In this way, exercise and rest are also your highest choices.

Living as what you really are, means asking yourself the question every moment, "What am I considering myself as right now?" If you remember your true nature in your everyday life, then you will naturally make the highest choices always. If you take decisions based on the belief that you are the body, then your decisions will not be the highest. For instance, then you may eat more than necessary when the food is delicious. You get entangled in the enjoyment of taste. But if you are living as what you are, you will eat only as much as the body requires. This is what is called as living as what you really are. You have to be aware of who you really are each moment, and the highest choice occurs spontaneously from this awareness.

You are making choices from morning to night. You simply have to be aware that each choice is the highest. Such supreme choices can be made only by being in the experience of Self. These choices will express the Self, express the truth. If you can live your life as what you actually are, then it is a supreme life.

18

Chanting and Experience of Self

Whenever I sit in silence for meditation, the image of Lord Krishna appears before my eyes. Often, I chant the name of Krishna throughout the day. But I want to know whether this is the right practice.

Every activity has a purpose. Some people chant mantras, some chant various names of Lord Shiva, Lord Krishna, Mother Goddess, or other gods. This chanting leads us to the experience of *being*, where the conviction arises: "I am not the body, I am this silence, this formless presence, which is always free and liberated." If this conviction is permeating your everyday life, then you are going in the right direction and the purpose of your meditation is also being fulfilled.

Every person is driven by different desires and goals. Some desire peace, while some want their fickle mind to come under control. If the mind, which is like a wild elephant, is chained by the neck, it wouldn't get stuck here and there unnecessarily. When a seeker grows and progresses beyond this state, they are then trained to reach the experience of Self.

By chanting all day, if the decisions of your life reflect that you are living as your true self, it means you are on the right track. Hence, you should mull over your present state by asking yourself, "Do the decisions of my life show that I am chanting Lord Krishna's name being my true self or being a separate individual?" If you are in sorrow or if your decisions keep changing because of others, then you need to realize that the purpose of your chanting or silence is not being fulfilled.

When you dip into silence after chanting, the purpose of the silence is to deeply imbibe, experience, and develop conviction on the teachings that you have heard during discourses. Your life will indicate that this is the right yardstick.

Reflect deeply to find the teachings that you haven't yet developed full conviction on. Let's consider an example. When a bucket gets filled with water, and the tap is still on, then the water starts overflowing in the bathroom, then out in the room, then all over your house, then outside the house, in your neighborhood, in your school, or in your workplace. You see its effect everywhere because the bucket was full. If it's not full, that means you need to fill your bucket. This implies that you need to work some more on developing full conviction of your true nature. When you are fully convinced, then it progressively shows in every aspect of your life.

Thus, all you need to understand now is that if chanting is augmenting your conviction, then you are on the right track and you can continue it. But if it's not, then you need some contemplation. Contemplate what change the chanting brings in your thinking and your decisions.

19
Recognize Your Fundamental Error

How should we utilize our free time? I also want to know, does the experience of *being* change when the state of the body changes?

The time you have today is more important than any other time of your life. Before old age sets in, your youth is nothing less than the biggest opportunity. Those who make best use of this valuable time always stay happy. To guarantee your happiness, you have to make the highest use of your time. Those, who lack the required understanding, indulge in useless activities to pass time. They eventually realize that time has passed them.

The state of the body is always changing. Sometimes it is fat, sometimes slim, sometimes it is heavy, at other times light. Changes do occur in the body, but it does not mean that the experience of *being* also changes. The more you look at the physical changes as a detached witness, the less you get entwined with the body. Eventually, any state of the body will make no difference to you. If the body feels heavy, you will say, "Yes, this happens. I have seen it so many times."

The experience of Self or *being* is always the same; it's just that it may sometimes seem intense and sometimes feeble due to changes in the body. For example, if you have kept your television in a well-lit room but the curtains are drawn, then the picture quality looks sharp. But when you open the curtains and the room is flooded with sunlight, the images on the television screen look fainter. The picture quality hasn't actually changed, but it appears so, because the light in the room has changed. The body is also like a room, in which the curtains of the senses are sometimes drawn and sometimes open. This is why you feel that the experience of *being* is intense at times and feeble at other times. The reality is, there's no difference in the experience of *being*. You have to look at these changing states without any attachment, i.e. with the understanding that this is not happening with you, it is happening with the body.

People often say, "Today I am tired," or "Today I have lots of energy." They don't realize that when they utter such words, how they gradually get entangled in those words. When a person says for the first time that he is tired, this is his first mistake. Doing this once may not matter much. But then the same mistake is repeated so many times that he forgets it's a mistake. The first or fundamental error has long been forgotten. This is why, instead of rectifying it, he is engaged in trying to correct all his secondary errors.

Suppose, you walk into someone's office without asking for permission, and then say, "May I sit on this chair or that one?" You would be told, "Your basic mistake is that you have entered without permission. So, first rectify that mistake." Likewise, a human being's basic mistake is to assume, "All that is happening with the body is happening with me." In other words, they associate with each and every event as if it's happening with them. They then repeat that error innumerable times. Since everyone around them is making the same mistake, they don't realize it's a mistake. Common sense says we should not punish ourselves for others' mistakes, but they do the exact opposite in this context.

For instance, you see someone on a street side whipping himself with a whiplash. You don't start doing the same to yourself, because you don't want the coins which he earns by doing so. It means you don't have to do what others are doing. Instead you should tell yourself, "If others are doing it, let them. But I know it's a mistake and so I am not going to copy them." If you stop making that error, it is possible that others also get the thought of not making that error. That's why, always be aware about the distinction between the body and the experience of *being*.

20
Importance of Discipline in Spirituality

How important is physical discipline for progressing on the path of spirituality?

An individual's spiritual journey can begin in two ways. The first way is to directly start with the Self and the second way is to start with the body. When you start with the body, it is essential to discipline the body. You have to train the body to be ready for that state in which you can reach the Self and experience it. It is to address this necessity that arrangements have been made in society, such as going to the temple in the morning and sitting for prayer and worship.

If someone has the habit of sitting every morning, whether for prayer or any other ritual, this habit helps when they begin the practice of meditation. Such people sit in meditation just as they would sit for prayer because they already have that habit and discipline. The purpose of cultivating the habit of praying is that, when it's time to begin the practice of meditation, one can easily start right away. In the olden days, the daily ritual of worship and prayer was taught to people so that they could develop discipline in their bodies. However, with time, the original intention was forgotten and only the ritual remained.

People forgot to progress to meditation and access the Self, only rituals continued. This is just like a person who always polishes his shoes but never begins his journey. Most people make this blunder and this is a huge blunder. Therefore, instead of engaging in such rituals and committing this mistake, it would be more beneficial if a person acquires spiritual knowledge and practices it while walking, talking, working, and at various other times.

Those who adopt the second way—of beginning their spiritual journey with the body—would want every aspect of their body to be disciplined. Be it being able to see with a clear vision, proper listening, exact pronunciation of words, or the ability to memorize. Later, when they have to remember the truth, all these qualities will be useful. Otherwise, most people totally neglect their memorization skills as soon as they have finished their school or college. That's why, as their age increases, people should engage in such practices and training once again. For example, some day you can decide: "Today I will memorize all the seven wonders of the world in proper order." Even though it's not important to remember this piece of information, it helps to exercise your brain.

People are made to practice the chanting of mantras, so that they can develop the habit of remembering the truth. Even if someone has not understood the meaning of something, the habit of chanting enables them to remember it. And so, when the time comes for the real chanting, meaning when they begin to know the experience of *being*, then an external mantra such as "Who am I?" also helps them to remember the inner experience.

In this way, all these habits are useful, but the danger is that with passage of time, the practices themselves become the goal, and the person becomes *sattvik* and gets stuck in them.

You may be aware that there are three *gunas* or fundamental natures, which are present in all human beings in varying proportions. These natures make up the disposition of every individual. In every body, one of these natures is dominant. The first one is *tamoguna*, which is a state of darkness, inertia, ignorance, and materialism. Second is *rajoguna*, the state of energy, action, ambition, and attachment. Third is *sattvaguna*, the state of balance, harmony, discipline, and intelligence.

Getting stuck in *sattvik* nature implies not being able to move ahead from *sattva*. The real goal is to transcend the three *gunas* and reach the *gunateet* (beyond the three natures) state, which is the original state of the Self.

Those who are sattvik are always showered with praises, and hence they often don't understand that they still have to progress ahead. If you examine all the characters of the *Mahabharata*, you will notice that some are stuck in *tamoguna*, some in *rajoguna*, and some in *sattvaguna*. There are very few characters who have reached beyond *sattva*; Lord Krishna is in the *gunateet* state. Discipline will surely help you reach the *sattvik* state, but the danger of getting stuck in that state is also always present.

At times, a question arises in an individual's mind, "Why should I pray? Why do I need to ask for true wisdom? I already have it. I know the truth because every morning I sit in the temple and study the scriptures." Only a so-called wise person gets such questions because they are not aware of the importance of prayer. The habit of prayer helps every person to progress on the path of spirituality. In fact, every person should have enough inner power to be able to pray. You should continue to pray for ultimate and unbroken bliss.

If you have practiced a lot on prayer, the next scene will automatically appear. It's very good if you are being able to understand the Guru's teachings about the experience of *being*. But if you are unable to understand, then you are given certain activities to discipline your body-mind. Thus, if your body-mind is totally disciplined, it will most definitely help you to progress on the spiritual path.

21
Demonstration of Spirituality

Is it possible to practically demonstrate every spiritual teaching with experiments and proofs?

There are two methods of teaching: one is by explanation and the other is by demonstration. Demonstration is always possible because whatever you have understood, you can explain it and also demonstrate it. But the question remains, will the other person understand exactly what you are trying to convey?

In the game of 'dumb charades,' a player has to convey the name of a movie in gestures, and the partner has to guess that name. Suppose, the gesturing player says, "I have done what I could to demonstrate the name; I don't care if the other person gets it or not," then the game cannot be played properly. Because the important aspect of the game is, whether the partner understood the sign language or not? If the player can demonstrate the movie title in the right manner, then the partner may get it.

The same thing happens in spirituality. If you look from the spiritual perspective, then the lives of Lord Buddha and Lord Mahavira can be considered as a demonstration. However, the question is, what will people understand by reading or listening to their life stories? How will they take it? What meaning will they derive from it? Have they understood what was actually being conveyed, or something else?

There are certain aspects of the experience of *being* that can neither be put into words nor explained to others. But certain other aspects can even be scientifically demonstrated. For example, the effect of thoughts on a person's life can be demonstrated. Let's try to understand this through an example.

A Japanese author conducted an experiment in which glasses of water were exposed to different conditions. Soothing music and prayer were performed in the presence of one of the water samples. Whereas another sample was exposed to bad words and abuses. Then they were both frozen and observed under a microscope.

The molecules of the water, which was subjected to abuses, had formed haphazard and ugly patterns. Whereas the water molecules exposed to music, prayer, and gratitude, had organized themselves into beautiful designs like jewels. After these results, extensive research is being carried out to find out, which words of prayer create the best designs? What patterns does the uttering of words like 'peace' and 'love' create? What kind of abuses create the most unsightly patterns? All this is being proven by scientific methods.

Such experiments are possible for only some aspects of spirituality. The same approach does not apply to matters related to the experience of *being*. Although, the teachings being imparted to lead you to this experience, do have many aspects that can be explained and practically demonstrated. One of them is the Astral Body Healing Method*, in which your physical body is healed with the help of your astral body. Experiments have been performed to demonstrate its efficacy. Blood samples are collected before and after the experiment to prove the effect of the healing.

Thus, some things can be scientifically proven but some cannot,

---

*You can read more about this powerful method of healing in the book *The Source of Health* by Sirshree.

because our senses are not enough to understand them. Some things can be seen under a microscope, but many cannot. We should use and take advantage of things that can be scientifically proven, but we should not negate all those that cannot. There are many things that cannot be scientifically proven but are nonetheless true.

There have been many facts which science did not accept earlier, because it wasn't possible to prove them at that time. But later when it became possible to prove them, science accepted them. The reality is those things were as true before as they were later. In the olden days, people used to perform the purifying ritual of *havan*, in which they would recite mantras over the water in a cistern, and then sprinkle that water. At that time, there was no proof that the recital of mantras will have any effect on the water. After worship and prayer, when water is sprinkled on people, it means those beautiful patterns are being sprinkled on them. The faith of people in those days was so strong that they did not feel the need for any evidence.

In today's context, if you write the words 'Thank You' on the pot or container of your drinking water, the water begins to change its nature. This has been scientifically proven. But if an average person is asked to do this, they will say, "What nonsense! What can possibly happen by writing 'Thank you' on the water pot or water cooler?" Likewise, if you tell some teenagers that the words written on their T-shirt are affecting their body-mind, they will never accept it. But now you can declare to them that it is scientifically proven that whatever is written on their T-shirt will have a subtle effect on them. Likewise, if the words 'Happy thoughts' are written somewhere, they will definitely have their effect.

The point is, there are some ways in which spiritual teachings are being explained and demonstrated. You can understand some of these things, but not everything, because the aspects related to the experience of *being* cannot be understood in this way.

You know that science has its limits. What it can do today, it was unable to yesterday; and tomorrow it will do things which it cannot today. All the saints or masters who have given us spiritual knowledge, have in fact already told us *everything*. But most people have failed to fully receive that knowledge because of lack of receptivity. New experiments are always going on everywhere to increase the receptivity of people, so that they can easily receive and imbibe everything. You can also try out small experiments and give evidences to yourself. You should train yourself such that your life itself becomes a demonstration for others, your life becomes an inspiration for others to turn towards spirituality.

22

Let the Mind Get Effective Answers

The Self existed even before the universe was created, and at that time there was nothing else. Then how did the Self get the thought that it should create the world so that it can experience itself?

All such questions have been answered in spirituality, like, "How did everything begin?", "How did God get the thought of creating the world?", and so on. And actually, all those answers are not correct. But they are nothing less than grace, due to the simple reason that it is impossible to answer these questions in words, and yet answers have been given. The guru who gives these answers is fully aware that they are not correct. But these answers work, because their effect is such that it inspires the seeker to move towards the experience of Self. When a seeker experiences the formless Self, it is then that they realize, "Whatever I was told in words about this experience was sheer grace, because it is impossible to describe this experience. Without those words, I wouldn't have embarked on this journey of finding my true self."

This is the reason why all spiritual answers are different from one another. Some say a woman was created first, while others claim a man was created first. Yet others think that animals were created first, and then the contrast mind* was added to one of them to create humans. Although all these statements are false, yet they are effective, because they at least spur people to begin the process of seeking the truth and the source of everything—the limitless Self. If those answers were not given, the journey would have never begun. People get stuck in such questions first.

You may have noticed that in any social event, the first thoughts that enter people's minds are, what kind of clothes the guests are wearing, how this person is talking, why the seating arrangement is like this, and so on. Likewise, if a young man is speaking well, then people begin to inquire about him, whether he is married or single, where he is from, etc. If an important lecture is being delivered on a certain platform, then instead of listening to it, people usually start wondering about the lecturer, such as, who is she, where is she from, why has she been chosen to give the lecture, and so forth. If these questions are not answered, then people are unable to listen to anything else. And that's why some sort of answers are given, so that people can pay attention to the lecture. Such answers are effective because they succeed in silencing your mind. This is the reason that whenever questions related to spirituality and God are asked, different masters give different answers. Most of these answers satisfy the curiosity of people and encourage them to get down to the real work—spiritual practices to reach the Self.

There are some so-called intellectuals or "wise" ones who do nothing else but collect answers. They then compare the answers, doubt them, and criticize them, saying this answer is useless but that one is better. They spend their entire life doing this, but they are unable to achieve anything at the experiential level. This is because they don't understand it was simply grace that they were given those answers. It's unfortunate that they cannot stop themselves from finding faults even in them. Just like, while having a meal, some people keep pointing out some imperfections in the food, instead of just being grateful and enjoying it.

Some answers about God have been given since ancient times, such as, "First God was in the state of nothingness, and then he got the thought of creating the universe..." Whereas the truth is, unless there is a body, thoughts cannot arise. This is the most important role of the body. The Self created the body so that the Self could think, hence let the Self think what it wanted to think. This is told in the language of thoughts because it's the only language that humans understand. That's why it is said, "God thought of..." or "God had the thought that..." although the process of thinking became possible only after the human body came into existence. You too are asking this question only after getting a body. This is why the answers are given in the language of thoughts because there is no other option. In spite of all these limitations, you have been given so many answers, and hence you should consider it as grace.

Also, you need to understand that language was created after the world was created. Hence, language cannot express that which existed before the world was created. How can the entity that came after the world was created, be used to compare or judge that which was present before the world was created? The process of thinking started after the world came into existence. We know this language of thoughts and our scope is limited to this language, and hence it has to be used to give answers such as, "God made this universe to experience himself." The objective of this answer is to convey that this experience is going on even now. The purpose for which the universe was created is being fulfilled at this very moment too. Look at it with awareness. But people cannot comprehend this easily. All the answers given till date are actually God's jokes. The jokes have worked if you have become mature after listening to them, if you have become a positive thinker, and if you can perceive the truth behind all the happenings in this illusory world.

Language has limitations, and hence it can be understood only at the experiential level that whatever was told, was meant to enable us to reach this inner experience, even if it does not properly fit into those words. When you ponder upon this, you will realize that it is divine grace because that which cannot be described in words has been given some words. We cannot fathom or think about the formless, hence we have been told everything in the language of thoughts which we understand, so that we can at least contemplate on it.

The insight for you from this answer is that you get the exact lie that you need at a given time. Since you need that lie, it benefits you. Similarly, if you don't need a truth, it cannot help you. If it is given to you when you don't need it, it may even harm you. Suppose, you tell an adolescent, "You have failed in your exam, but the truth is, this is not happening *with* you, it is happening *for* you." Imagine how he would feel. He would be totally baffled. Instead, explain to him in the language of passing and failing, like, "Don't worry. I had failed twice, you at least have one more chance, so it's nothing to stress about." He will understand this easily, because it is being said in a language that he can relate to. The answer to your question has been given to you in the same way, but it can help you progress on the spiritual path. Therefore, reflect deeply on every answer and try to reach the ultimate truth.

---

*The contrast mind is that aspect of the mind which constantly splits everything into black or white, good or bad. It makes comparisons with others, judges, creates doubts, makes assumptions, wants everything to have a logical explanation, takes credit for everything, keeps thinking on events endlessly and unnecessarily leading to misery. It always swings between the past and future instead of staying in the present. It is this aspect of the mind which causes ego, hatred, malice, greed, envy, deceit, sorrow, boredom, etc. Thus, humans have the contrast mind as well as the straightforward instinctive mind. The contrast mind is present only in humans; animals possess only the instinctive mind.

Stabilization in the Self is possible only when the contrast mind surrenders to the Self with understanding. You can gain clarity on the contrast mind and how to make it peaceful and ready for surrender by reading the books *The Unshaken Mind* and *What To Do When The Mind Troubles You*, authored by Sirshree.

23
Understanding Paradoxical Wisdom

What is paradoxical wisdom and what are its benefits?

When we first hear the term 'paradoxical wisdom,' it seems incorrect. But on realizing its depth, it makes complete sense. In fact, the power of paradoxical wisdom is that it helps us to get rid of wrong assumptions and beliefs. Suppose, you feel that a particular person is your enemy. Then paradoxical wisdom will reveal that he is actually your friend. You have grown because of him and reached your goal because of him. If you ponder upon it, this truth will become obvious to you. But on first reading it, you may question, "How can the exact opposite be true?"

The egoistic mind will not agree. It wants to continue to exist and hence gives rise to thoughts such as, "I am right. This person is my enemy; he wishes bad for me. He does not respect me or care for me." The mind will try to prove it is right by saying, "See, this is how he behaved. It obviously means he wants to create hurdles in my path." The truth might be totally the opposite. This is the reason paradoxical knowledge is essential.

A student shared that he feels bad when a certain classmate scores more marks than him. You can understand that he believes that his classmate has left him behind by achieving better grades. Hence, he was given the paradoxical wisdom: "It's okay if someone else gets ahead of you, but don't ever let your thoughts get ahead. Your thoughts should not get the better of you." This knowledge made him realize that it was not his classmate but his own thoughts that were making him feel bad. He should not let them control him; rather he should control them, and thus get freedom from all his problems.

When a person is driving and suddenly someone overtakes him, he gets furious and bursts out, "That guy must be absolutely *crazy*! Look at the way he cut me off!" If this happens with you, remind yourself, "Let anyone overtake me, but my thoughts should not."

If you can take care of your thoughts, everything else will be taken care of. If you can actually do this, you will instantly see the results of paradoxical wisdom and wonder, "Wow! How did this happen? How did I get rid of the upsetting thoughts so quickly?!"

Accept and imbibe the power of paradoxical wisdom* and get liberated from unhappy thoughts arising from the events in life.

---

*You can read in detail about paradoxical wisdom in Sirshree's Hindi book *Virodhabhas Niyam*.

24

Introverts and Extroverts

What is the difference between introverts and extroverts?

This topic can be understood with the following statement: *The Self directed outward is the mind. The mind directed inward is the Self.* This means that the Self goes out and becomes the mind; and the mind comes within and becomes the Self.

In spirituality, more importance is given to becoming an introvert first. Becoming an introvert means, when you are looking at an incident taking place, first observe what is happening within you on watching that incident. For instance, if someone made a sour face when you said something, then what happened inside you? How bad did you feel and how long did that feeling last? If you deeply contemplate such questions and reach the experience of *being*, you are becoming an introvert.

Extroverts are the total opposites. They want to see the thoughts occurring within them in the other person too. Suppose, an extrovert meets someone for the first time and gets a thought: "This woman is bad." He then starts looking for the bad in every little action of that woman—whether she is walking, talking, laughing, crying, or anything else. In effect, he is using his inner thoughts to live his outer life. Whereas the introvert uses thoughts from outside to go within himself. He sees them as a mirror.

The introvert thinks and then talks, whereas the extrovert talks and then thinks. If an extrovert lady wants to think of what she has to do next, she will not think in her mind, she will say it aloud: "Clothes have to be ironed, kids have to be sent to school, cooking is yet to be done… when will all this get done?... How long will this go on?" By saying this aloud, she is thinking of a solution. If such people are asked to think all of this quietly, they cannot. They need someone to talk to, so that they can figure out the solution to their problems. Whereas, introverts think of all this within their minds. Quite often, it happens that until they can think and then speak, the time is gone. On the other hand, an extrovert often speaks out something without thinking that hurts people, who may then carry that hurt for years. Thus, both extremes are harmful.

When a person avoids both extremes and learns to always stay on the middle path, meaning when they fully mature in this spiritual practice of staying in the middle, they reach the fine line between the outer and inner. This means they learn to stay at their center, their heart, their *tejasthan* or the bright place where the Self connects with the body. From this place, it is easy for them to go within and also to go out for carrying out their daily activities. Hence, it would be highly beneficial if you too can cultivate the habit of going to your *tejasthan* in every situation and contemplating.

25
Ways to Develop the Intellect

What should we do to develop our intellect?

If you want to develop and make something stronger, then you must use it more and more. When the right hand is used more, it becomes much stronger than the left, and vice versa. There is a saying, "Use it or lose it." This means if you don't use something, you will lose it. This is why exercise is important, so that all your body parts remain active and become strong. The brain is also a part of the body, which needs to be active. When you use it continuously, it gets the required exercise. This is the beauty of the human body.

Very often, the brain does not get much exercise after finishing school or college. Hence, you need to put in some conscious efforts. When you solve a puzzle, it gets some exercise. When you have to solve some problem of your everyday life, and if there are multiple possible solutions, try to find the best one. This will exercise your brain.

There are many methods to develop your brain or intellect. Suppose you are going to cook a dish, then tell yourself, there are ten ways of cooking it. When you challenge yourself by saying, "I have to find the best way of doing this, or a new method of doing this," then this is an exercise for your intellect.

When people don't think of bringing about some newness, they start doing things in the same manner all the time. Like someone always prepares meals in the same way. If a newness has to be introduced, one will have to use some creativity. If you are cooking a dish, then count every little step of the process. For instance, you keep the pot on the stove, say one, then you pick up the tomato, say two, you cut the tomato, say three. By the time you reach hundred, your dish will be done. This is a new and creative method of cooking. The next day, take this count up to two hundred, meaning you have to count even the minutest steps. On the first day, you did not count every single step because your awareness was relatively less. The next day, you will be counting with more awareness. And by doing so, you won't get time to think about unnecessary things. You won't be mulling or complaining about your neighbor, because you are aware of your every action. In this way, you are happy, the one who eats is happy, your brain gets some exercise, you can stay in the present, and your awareness also increases.

Whatever activity you are doing, think about how it can be done differently. You will have to develop the habit of asking yourself, "What can be another method of doing this?" If you want, you can even think of different ways of taking a bath. You can find at least seven different methods, if not more. When you do this, then even the task of bathing, which used to be boring, will become fun. Just remember that you only need to tap into your creativity to usher in some newness and freshness.

Whatever work you do, it always exercises your brain. The more you exercise it, the more your intellect will open up and develop. When you continue to think and use new methods of doing things, everything will get done easily.

In your daily life, you get so many opportunities to exercise your brain that you really don't need to do anything more. You only have to ask questions. Asking questions strengthens your intellect. Because then you have to think from a different perspective. For example, someone asks you, "Other than sitting, can you think of one such use of a chair, which no one has thought before?" When you are asked such questions, there's no option but to think anew. Just like kids have thought of a new use of a chair. When they play cricket, they use it instead of stumps. When you start thinking of new ways of using an ordinary object like a chair, then your creative faculty gets some practice. If you are awake and aware, then you get plenty of such opportunities in your routine life.

You can ask yourself, "When I get negative thoughts, what should I do? I will find a hundred ways of dealing with it." With a challenge like this, you will automatically get flooded with new ideas. When you search for a hundred ways, you will at least find ten. As you ponder over those ten ways, you will find even more ways. On the other hand, if you had thought that "one day" you will think of a solution to your problem, you might have never got so many methods to deal with it. But when you tell yourself that you have to find ten different solutions for a given problem today, then it starts happening spontaneously.

When you start counting every little action while doing something, as the numbering progresses, you may feel that thoughts have totally stopped, and you cannot think of anything. But soon you will find a totally new dimension, something out of the box! By the time you can count again from one to ten, you will easily get a lot of ideas. This may seem a bit difficult initially, but it will go on getting easier when you practice regularly.

SECTION III

The Path to Freedom

26
The Path of Freedom from Negative Emotions

Sometimes in our life, we suppress certain emotions in our heart. Some people, for example, do not usually express their feelings of anger and violence, and stifle them within. What can be done to dissolve such undesirable emotions?

People initially use various techniques to achieve freedom from undesirable tendencies like anger and violence. Emotional Freedom Technique (EFT) and Bach Flower Therapy (BFT) are two such methods to deal with suppressed emotions. These methods are quite popular and can provide relief from emotional issues to a large extent. Apart from these, there is a meditation technique called Releasing Meditation* which helps you to let go of all suppressed emotions. In this way, you can move ahead step by step.

Listening deeply to discourses on the ultimate truth and contemplating them can liberate you from every suppressed emotion as well as tendency. Understanding of the ultimate truth makes you realize that these are nothing but accumulated negative feelings in your mind, and you have to learn the art of witnessing them with awareness.

---

*You can read in depth about Releasing Meditation and how to achieve liberation from all negative emotions in the book *Emotional Freedom Through Spiritual Wisdom* by Sirshree.

Suppose, you are standing in front of a mirror and there is unnecessary design on its surface which hinders you from seeing a clear image of yourself. Here the mirror represents your body-mind, the design symbolizes your tendencies, and the image of yourself means the experience of your true, formless self. What's amazing is that if you look at the design in the right manner, it will spontaneously start melting away. Otherwise, instead of looking at your true self, you may get stuck in thoughts such as, "The design on my mirror is better than the design on that person's mirror." This is how people get stuck in tendencies.

Spirituality teaches you the art of witnessing. If you go deeper into the practice of spirituality, you will develop this art even more. Whatever emotion arises in you, you don't have to suppress it, nor do you have to aggressively express it on someone else. The understanding behind this should be, "Emotions are in the body-mind and not in my true self." With this perception, you will notice that gradually the effect of the emotions is diminishing. Day by day, you will feel the difference that these negative emotions don't trouble you as much as before. You will have to give adequate time for these emotions to dissolve completely.

In various situations, the suppressed emotions within you like hopelessness, boredom, or stress get a chance to surface and you begin to feel them on your body. At such times, just look at the emotions with awareness. These emotions that are being experienced at the physical level imply that the body is giving you feedback. For instance, when you eat very spicy food, your tongue instantly starts burning. This is the body's feedback and is essential. If you don't get this feedback, you will continue to eat the spicy dish as you find it delicious. Since too much spice is not good for the body, it gives feedback, because of which you stop eating it.

By making the negative feelings evident, the body is doing its job perfectly. Hence, if depression is being felt, don't enhance it by repeatedly thinking, "Why am I depressed?" Instead, you can think, "My body is doing an excellent job and so should I. Together we will accomplish some great work." As your understanding of your true self increases and you continue to witness your emotions as separate from you, then the unease and turmoil inside you will cease. Thereafter, you won't do anything apprehensively but rather happily because there is only joy on the path as well as the destination. You have to look at everything only with happiness. When you can do this, then feeling depressed over depression, feeling unhappy about unhappiness, feeling angry about your anger, or regretting your regrets, will stop.

Thus, when you learn the right way to look at each negative emotion, it won't overpower you. When you develop the conviction that this emotion is not occurring with you but with the body, then the influence of that emotion will gradually decline.

27
Surrendering the Ego Through Unconditional Devotion

The ego within me is the obstacle in seeking the truth. How can I achieve freedom from this ego?

To begin with, stop serving the ego. This means don't fulfil the desires of the ego, which wants to establish a separate identity for itself. The ego always tries to stand out. "How can I look different from others?" It persistently tries a variety of ideas to achieve this. It is while serving the ego that you resort to deceit, assumptions, envy, jealousy, hatred, and lies. If someone hurts your ego, then your ego won't rest until it makes you do something in retaliation. Hence, we need to stop serving the ego in this manner. Don't live like ice by separating yourself from water (God), but live like water (which you are in reality).

Prayer can eliminate the ego. The mind harbors the ego that it has achieved so much till date and hence it can achieve everything. But it has no idea that there are a lot of secrets which will be revealed only when it receives divine grace. Just like you cannot catch a magician's tricks until the magician wishes to, similarly, in order to know God's secrets, one needs to surrender to God. Only when the ego is ready to bow down, do the secrets begin to unfold one by one. Silence of the ego allows the truth to come forth. Prayer is readiness for the ego to bend, where it understands that there is nothing greater than divine grace.

When an egoist realizes that there is a power higher than them, they can then easily surrender to that power. This surrender becomes a prayer. Thereon, they don't have to ask for or snatch anything from anyone in their life. They begin to get whatever they want without asking for it. Their life blooms with happiness.

Devotion plays an important role in the annihilation of ego. First of all, it is important to understand your perspective of wisdom, karma, and devotion. Generally, people think these three are separate entities. Very few people are able to recognize that karma arising from wisdom is true devotion.

If you are giving importance only to wisdom, then you need to understand that devotion plays a crucial role in the surrender of ego, and hence it is essential to cultivate devotion. If the mind develops devotion, it will stop creating doubts on the truth and also stop taking credit for anything. This will give rise to feelings of wonder and praise for God, which will enhance your joy, since all these feelings are connected with devotion. As devotion rises, the ego is able to surrender itself.

In family relations, when the ego surrenders due to love, there is always a hidden desire. For example, a person thinks, "If I do this, then my children will respect me and care for me in my old age." Thus, there is always a condition for the ego to surrender, but in true devotion, the ego surrenders unconditionally.

When devotion deepens, the mind lets go of all its doubts on the truth. You can then understand by your own experience that the ego *can* be surrendered, but you have to stop delving into doubts. *You can attain the truth by listening to truth discourses.* If you can develop conviction on this statement, then supreme faith and reverence awakens in your heart. Be totally open to receive the supreme truth and enjoy the transformation being brought about by devotion in your life.

Always render service with devotion in your heart, so that the mind does not get stuck in just being an intellectual. Continue to follow the practice of devotion until your heart opens fully. Whenever you are singing a hymn, pay attention to whether it is reaching your heart or not. Because if it reaches your heart, you can directly connect to the Self or the divine source within. From the source, the expression of wonder, praise, joy, laughter, and tears of devotion becomes possible. Don't stop any of these from happening. This is the power of devotion. Neither halt it nor use any force against it. The ego will automatically surrender with the power of devotion*.

---

*You can read in depth about devotion in Sirshree's books *Essence of Devotion* and *100% Devotion*.

28

Freedom from Negative Tendencies And Patterns

What should we do to break our tendencies and patterns?

One may listen to truth discourses from any source, but what's important is that it should help them in achieving freedom from their behavioral patterns and tendencies. This is the purpose of spiritual knowledge. After receiving the right knowledge, one can also become instrumental for one's family and friends in attaining the truth.

Devotion also helps you to break free from negative tendencies and patterns. Suppose, fifty events including major and minor ones occur in your life on an average day. If you are trying to imbibe devotion in your everyday life, you will ask yourself, "Have I been able to give a different and better response in at least four or five events?" Such small steps can go a long way in dislodging your patterns, which increases the possibility of breaking them completely. When you can give a new and softer response in spite of your aggressive tendencies, that is when new possibilities open up for you.

Devotion has two main aspects: *unconditional* and *in spite of*. If you encounter a situation in which someone is behaving negatively with you, you have to ask yourself, "Am I able to give a devotion-filled response *in spite of* this behavior?" Learning from such simple experiments enables major transformations. Repeated blows can shatter even the toughest rocks. You have to do the same. Continue to strike at your deep-rooted patterns with small experiments.

You can also take help of prayers to get rid of your tendencies. When your prayers are clear and in one specific direction, your life becomes easy, natural, and joyful. Continue to pray in one direction for your patterns to break. When your prayers are split into many directions, then the happenings around you get a chance to overpower you and your prayers begin to change.

Quite often such things happen in your home or outside that cause your thoughts to stray in wrong directions. That's when prayers assist you in giving a proper direction to your thoughts. This change is positive and essential. When a certain idea enters your thoughts, it becomes possible for it to get manifested in reality.

Thus, unconditional devotion, the habit of experimenting, and single-pointed prayers will help you to achieve freedom from your tendencies.

29
Thirst for Freedom and Spiritual Strength

Whenever I close my eyes, I connect with the Self within and stay with it. But as soon as my eyes open, all the tendencies and stories of the mind take over. How can I achieve freedom from these? Is there a special technique for this?

The more intense your thirst for freedom, the more easily you will be able to transcend the tendencies and stories of the mind.

First, you will have to learn to properly control these tendencies, because it is only when they go beyond control that your mind says, "Now something needs to be done. Otherwise things are going on okay. I can certainly tolerate this much amount of pain and sorrow." But ask yourself, "Do I want to live my entire life suffering from sorrow caused by the stories of my mind? If I spend all my days in this manner, would there be any meaning to my life?" If you continue to suffer all your life, then at the end, the question is bound to arise: "Why did I continue to make the same mistakes even after attaining wisdom?" Because this implies that it made no difference in your life whether you received wisdom or not.

If continuing with the mind's stories and repeating the same mistakes is acceptable to you, then let your life continue as is. But if this kind of life is not acceptable to you, then pray earnestly for the kind of life you want. Make it clear whether you want to live with the mind's stories and tendencies *or* with the truth.

Praying sincerely that you *really* want to live your life with the truth will strengthen your faith and resolve. This will create the right circumstances in your life. You will get the right *satsang* (company of truth seekers), the right discourses, and the right books which are necessary for liberation. Everything will automatically begin to become possible. What used to take a lot of effort earlier will then happen effortlessly. But for this to happen, your desire for liberation should be genuine and strong.

"I want to live as who I truly am." Continue to repeat this prayer. To begin with, your prayer can be, "I want to live most of the time as who I truly am." If you cannot live as your true self all the time, then you may do so as much as possible. If you drink water every two hours, you can also remember the truth every couple of hours. Ask yourself, "How often is it possible for me to remember the truth?" Then accordingly remind yourself of the truth as much as possible.

In this way if you can pass the first stage, then it will become possible to pass the second stage as well, which is living as your true self always. That's why you need to clearly tell yourself what's the minimum you can work to achieve this goal, and then stick to it. When you take up small goals and manage to achieve them, your spiritual strength will increase. Hence, strengthen your desire for ultimate liberation and increase your spiritual strength. Your intellectual power has already increased, because that's what made it possible for you to reach the path of truth. Now make a plan for everything you need to do for achieving your goal and follow that plan. Then no story or tendency can obstruct your path.

30

Freedom from Fear

Just last week something happened that made me very scared. Fearful thoughts totally overwhelmed me and I was shaken to the core. The stress got so bad that I had to take medicine to reduce my hypertension. Lack of sleep is making it difficult to focus on anything. What should I do to get rid of this fear?

First of all, understand that the thoughts of fear which have arrived will also leave. In fact, they have arrived only to leave, hence there is no need to be afraid of them.

Awaken yourself so that you can achieve freedom from them. This state, which is scaring you, is temporary and a result of your prayers till date. But unless you disable this fearful state, you may live in this state for years on end. Then you will enter the next stage where your mind will create even more fear.

That's why it is important that with the first thought of fear, the second thought should also arise. Suppose, a thought pops up in your mind: "Something bad is going to happen." Then another thought should also arise: "No, I can get rid of it." Although both these thoughts are yours, you have to give power to the thought that you believe in.

Fear has emerged only to awaken you. It has arrived to show how ready you are to handle situations.

"I can deal with this... I can handle this, as I have done so several times before." Repeat such encouraging words in your mind. When the mind wonders, "Will this fearful thought actually manifest?", tell it, "Only that will happen which is according to God's plan for me." Keep on affirming this to yourself. Also tell yourself, "I am going to turn this fear into a stepping stone for my internal growth. I have bought this fear on rent so that I may recognize and manifest the courage inherent within me."

Just as you need a black board to write with a white chalk, likewise, you need to get fear temporarily in order to experience courage. This fear is an opportunity; make good use of it.

Learn to release your fearful thoughts by telling yourself that you got to let go of fear because better days are waiting for you—days when you can be very happy. You have to keep recalling the feeling of happiness. If you keep recollecting fearful thoughts, then their power to cling to you will go on increasing.

If you take these precautions, then this state of fear* will also pass.

---

*You can read in detail about how to achieve liberation from fear in the book *Freedom from Fear, Worry, Anger* by Sirshree.

SECTION IV

Meditating to Attain The Right Understanding of Meditation

31
Meditate with the Right Understanding

You have told us to meditate daily for 20 minutes. This is surprising because I have been meditating for two hours every day since the last ten years, but nothing much has happened. Is it possible to connect with the Self with only 20 minutes of meditation?

The right understanding of meditation is more important than the time spent in meditation. Even 20 minutes of meditation done with the right understanding can be very beneficial.

Meditation can lead us to the experience of Self in the wakeful state. When an individual sleeps for 8-10 hours, then if the time spent in dreaming is left aside, they are in the supreme state of Self during the rest of the duration of sleep. But as soon as their eyes open in the morning, the same old individual wakes up. There is no difference in their understanding despite being in the experience of Self for so long. They are still stuck in the same wrong beliefs and sorrows. They continue to do everything in the same manner as before going to sleep.

If a person reaches the experience of Self by practicing meditation with the right understanding, then even a short time is sufficient. People spend hours in meditation without the right understanding and then share their stories with each other. "Today, this is what happened in meditation. Last time, something else had happened; I wonder why that did not happen today…" This shows their lack of understanding, because they remain stuck in superficial experiences, leaving aside the actual purpose of meditation.

People who practice meditation get all kinds of experiences. Some may see rays of light, some may behold scenes of heaven, some feel a certain chakra has activated, some may say this time they experienced *khechari kriya* and felt as if they tasted nectar, some say they could focus on their third eye, and so on. People narrate all kinds of experiences related to meditation, but they don't stop to think whether these experiences have brought any change in their false beliefs or in their conviction that they are the formless and limitless self. This conviction is more important than anything else in meditation.

Suppose, Rama, a male actor, is playing the female character of Shakuntala on stage. After playing the role, if he steps down from the stage but continues to consider himself as Shakuntala, you would say, "Hey, you are not Shakuntala, you are Rama." If, in response, he says, "Yes, I understand that I am Shakuntala," you are going to be baffled. Because now he believes himself to be that character. In fact, he is unwilling to understand who he really is.

The same mistake sometimes occurs during meditation. Irrespective of the time you spend in meditation, the real purpose is to deepen the conviction of what you are and what you are not. If meditation is practiced with this understanding and intention, then even a little time can work wonders. However, this doesn't mean that someone who can practice for more than 20 minutes should not do so. You can practice for whatever maximum time is possible for you, but it should be at least 20 minutes, because this will wonderfully expand your understanding of the Self.

During meditation, you will experience what you have listened during discourses. This will build your conviction that what is being said in discourses *is* the truth. Then the truth will permeate your decisions and actions. Your words may not reveal who you truly are, but your decisions do. Your decisions reflect whether you are practicing meditation with the right understanding or not.

If someone is sitting for hours in meditation but only their ego is getting strengthened, it means they are not practicing in the right manner. On the other hand, if one is meditating with understanding even for a short time but its transformative effect is seen in their decisions, then their practice is correct. After such meditation sessions, in every action, you will remember who you truly are and who you are living as. In the outer world, everyone has a role to play, like that of a spouse, a parent, an employee, a boss, a neighbor, etc. But your choices while playing these roles will express who you truly are and who you consider yourself to be while making those choices. Thus, your decisions will represent you.

The main purpose is that by practicing meditation, your conviction that you are not the body, should increase. This miracle can happen in a short time. Hence, always meditate with the right understanding*.

---

*You can read the books *Complete Meditation—222 Questions, You are Meditation,* and *100% Meditation* by Sirshree to gain complete understanding of true meditation.

32
Awareness of the Body

Sometimes, we don't lose awareness of the body during meditation. Then what should we do?

It's not a big deal if awareness of the body does not disappear during meditation. As you get better at meditation, gradually body awareness will begin to disappear on its own.

But the desire to lose body awareness is in itself a big hurdle in meditation. Because then you want a special experience from meditation. Losing body awareness is not the purpose of meditation, but simply a bonus. People get caught up in this bonus. If you think about it, you do lose your body awareness every time you sleep, but this does not make you happy on waking up. This means, if the understanding of your true self does not increase, then there is no benefit from disappearance of body awareness.

People get various experiences in meditation, but that doesn't benefit them and only boosts their ego. Due to ignorance, they believe that these superficial experiences are the real benefit; but these are actually just the mind's desire. You should realize your true self and develop conviction on it. This is the actual purpose of meditation and it should serve this purpose. This is more important than anything else.

You cannot meditate properly due to the mind's desires. As a result, you may be engulfed by various thoughts, miserable feelings, aches and pains in legs, back, etc. during meditation. That's why, before you sit in meditation, it is important to tell yourself, "If any aches and pains occur, I will witness them for a while and then ask myself whether they are happening to me or to my body." If the answer is that it's occurring with your body, then ask yourself, "Can I continue to sit in meditation for some time, in spite of this pain?" Then you can stretch your legs once and get back to your meditation once again.

Due to the mind's desires, people tend to get lost in their imaginations about meditation. They believe that their meditation session is successful only if they lose awareness of their body or if they see a light. This is merely an assumption of the mind, hence don't get trapped by it. If thoughts were going on during meditation and your mind could not focus, don't get dejected. Instead, harbor the understanding that such meditation sessions are preparing you to move ahead.

When the rope tied to a well constantly rubs against the underlying stone, after some time it creates a mark on it and gradually an indentation. Regular walking on a rocky hill also creates a path on it. So, just start practicing meditation, and gradually a path leading deeper within will start forming. However, most of the times, instead of walking on this path, people say that no one has walked on this path, so they won't either. They don't understand that unless they start walking, the path will not be formed.

On the other hand, there are people who simply start walking with the thought: "No matter what, I am going to sit in meditation." Such people pave a new path and also reach the destination.

A person goes to a temple, rings the bell hanging inside, comes out and listens to its echo. The echo makes him feel that the temple is calling him and he goes back inside the temple. You have to do the same in meditation. As soon as you sit in meditation, you have to listen to the echo of the Self within you and then go inside. Otherwise, the mind will say, "There is too much commotion within, I wouldn't like to go in there... that man is looking at me angrily... this one is staring at me... that person is doing this to me... and this is happening in my life... so how can I go within?"

Whatever excuses the mind presents, you still have to go inside and ring the bell; meaning you have to know the Self within you through meditation. Then you can come outside and listen to the echo, which means, when you get into your routine activities after meditation, your attention should continue to be on the Self. Only then you will reach the Self in the true sense.

33

Quality is More Important than Quantity of Meditation

If so much can be attained with just 20 minutes of meditation along with some discourses and contemplation on the truth, then can we speed up the process of attaining the truth by doing this full-time?

The most important factor to attain the truth is quality. If someone practices meditation without the proper understanding, then their meditation doesn't develop quality. After meditating regularly for at least 20 minutes, your conviction of your true nature gradually goes on strengthening. This is why you are advised to practice for minimum 20 minutes. By listening to discourses here, you have understood that it's possible to attain the truth in a short time rather than in many decades or many births. This is why you increased the duration of your meditation, so that you can attain the truth as soon as possible.

You have learnt here that the way to attain the truth is by remaining within the triad of truth, which consists of listening to truth, service for truth, and devotion for truth. Your thought of abiding in this triad for 18 hours a day is very auspicious indeed. In the beginning, seekers are instructed to practice meditation for 20-30 minutes, so that they will at least start practicing. If someone is able to do this regularly, then as they start understanding true meditation, they can increase the duration. You can keep things in a container only if it is empty. This 20-30 minutes of meditation for everyone is akin to emptying the container of one's body-mind, so that the truth can be poured into it. Hence, if you wish to, you may increase the duration.

By consistently practicing meditation every day, after some time, you will find that you are living throughout the day with the conviction that you are not the body. In this state, you are always in meditation even if you aren't physically seated in meditation. Without listening to the truth, you are listening to the truth. This is because whatever you hear from anyone, you will immediately spot the illusion of what is being said and discern the truth behind it. Thus, you would be listening to the truth while hearing anything that anyone is saying to you. This is the greatest benefit that you get from meditation.

For example, someone tells you, "Today is such a dull day." But you will get the thought: "It's a perfect day." That person may be right according to his belief system. However, the truth is that each day is perfect. Every moment is a scene created by God and hence it cannot get better than it is. Everything is just as it is meant to be. It is so perfect that we cannot add or subtract anything from it. Thus, in effect, this thought has made you 'listen to the truth.'

Whatever anyone says, you will listen only to the truth, and you won't even have to try for that. To attain this state, it would certainly be beneficial to increase the duration of practicing meditation, listening to discourses, and contemplation. But you won't need this calculation all your life, because after some time, you will notice that you are living as your true self all day long. Then meditation will be happening automatically, whether you are sitting, walking, or in any other position. The condition that meditation should be done only in the seated position would no longer apply. But it's mandatory to sit regularly for some time when you are a beginner, so as to progress in your practice.

If your present level of understanding is inspiring you to spend more time in the pursuit of truth in order to attain it faster, then definitely go ahead and do it. Keep in mind all the aspects and practice meditation, listen to the truth, read, and contemplate it. But this calculation will change with time. Later the question, "Should I stay with the truth part-time or full-time?" won't even arise, because only truth will remain. When the 'individual' or the false 'I' disappears, you spontaneously start living in the truth every moment. Earlier, the question used to arise, "Who am I?" but later it will change to, "Who was that?" You would question and wonder about your false 'I' because you would then be living as who you truly are—the formless and limitless Self.

At present, there are still several corners of your life which are in darkness and need to be brought to light. By increasing the time for your spiritual practices, you can soon be free from those dark corners. Giving more time will certainly help. After attaining complete understanding of truth, when you attend discourses, it won't be because you need them, but it would be simply for expressing wonder, praise, and bliss of the truth. In the beginning, one does everything in the pursuit of truth, and later for the sheer joy of it.

34

Clarity of Meditation

How should we look at the clouds of confusion and ambiguity in our life?

When you find clouds covering the moon, you know that it will be visible after some time when the clouds drift away. Thus, all your attention is on the moon. Although the dark clouds are looming in your vision, you involuntarily try to look behind them. If you see just a sliver of light on one side, your gaze falls upon it, even if the moon has come out or not. This means you are aware of the moon even before you can see it.

Similarly, if your attention is fixed on the Self (moon), then any negative or positive thoughts (black or white clouds) would make no difference to you. This is called as stabilization or getting established in the Self. In unawareness, you focus on those thoughts, thereby lending them your power. As soon as your awareness rises, these thoughts begin to fade. You have to try to keep your focus on the Self behind the thoughts.

The cloud's appearance will give you a fair idea about how long it will take for the moon to shine forth. Then you wouldn't want to waste a single moment; if you get even a fleeting glimpse of the moon, you would catch it. In whatever fraction of time is available between two passing clouds (between thoughts), you would fully take in the light of the moon (the experience of Self).

This is the way you should look at the confusions or problems in your life. Always try to see the moon of truth behind them. By doing so, they cannot take you away from the truth. There is no difficulty or ambiguity that has the power to hide the truth for long. The truth is always there for you to see—all you need is awareness for it.

35

Experience of Self In Every Moment

Does the experience of Self that we get during meditation stop after the meditation session, or does it continue? If it continues, then why don't we feel it?

When you practice meditation consistently, you will gradually develop the conviction that the experience you had during meditation is continuing even after the meditation session, in fact it is present all the time. There wasn't any noise or activity during meditation, and that's why the experience of Self was very clear. After you finish the meditation session and get busy in your daily chores, there is noise around you and the conducive meditative atmosphere is absent. Hence, you are unable to feel the experience of Self at that time. But gradually, as your receptivity, tuning, and subtleness increases, you will be able to clearly experience the Self even in a noisy atmosphere.

Let us understand this by considering the example of two songs that are playing at the same time. One song is playing softly and the other is loud. Initially, you cannot hear the softer song. Then if the loud song is turned off for some time, your attention goes to the softer song. If the loud song starts playing again, you feel as if the softer song has stopped, whereas actually you are unable to catch the subtle sound. If you really want to hear it even when the loud song is playing, then you will resolve: "I am going to practice listening to the softer song in spite of the noise." Thus, you gradually start hearing and enjoying the soft song, and thereafter your attention will be on it most of the times.

This is what happens during meditation. When you are in the outside world, you listen to the noise of the body and the senses, and hence you feel that the subtle experience of Self has stopped. The truth is, this experience never stops. When your practice of meditation becomes consistent, you will understand that the experience of Self is always going on. It is this conviction that will stabilize you in the Self.

36

The Art of Living In this Illusory World

At home, at work, or in society at large, there are always lots of things going on related to this illusory world (*maya*), and I get drawn into it. What should I do in such situations?

Before trying to understand the right way to live in this illusory world *(maya)*, you need to identify where you often go wrong. The mistake that people usually make is that *after* they get angry, they ask, "Now what should I do?" They ask this question whenever anger or some problem arises; whereas they should be preparing for it well in advance. Suppose, somebody is feeling very thirsty and then asks, "Where should I dig a well?" He will be told, "There's not much you can do now. Whatever had to be done, should have been done before you felt thirsty. You should have started digging much earlier."

Your question is similar. Don't do anything when you have already dived into *maya*, but after going home, you need to ponder over some crucial points: "What do I actually gain by getting involved in things related to maya? Is this what I have come to do on Earth? Is this what I will be doing all my life? How long will this continue?" Then decide exactly how long you are going to indulge in maya. If your decision is six months or some other specific period, that's fine. But then after that period, totally stop getting drawn into maya. In this way, you have to plan in advance. Thereafter, the next time a similar situation lures you, you will become aware and easily get out of that situation by making some excuse and leaving that scene.

If you try to think while you are immersed in *maya*, "What should I do? Should I do this or should I do that?", you won't be able to figure out exactly what to do. There is very little time to think in that vulnerable moment. Hence, don't do anything at that time and also don't *not* do anything. Just witness what is happening and observe what you are doing in this maya. Become a witness of your own behavior, because only if you become aware of your wrong actions will the possibility of getting rid of them arise.

You can plan much in advance: "What would I do when people in my office indulge in maya? Or what can I do so that my presence can inspire people to come out of maya?" If you can do this, it is possible that by seeing your steadfastness in truth, someone may start thinking that they too can live like you.

For example, you are watching a cricket match on the television. You get excited when the players hit a four or a six, and feel bad when they get out. Similarly, while indulging in maya, observe yourself: "What is happening with me and when? When do I get excited? When do I get entangled in my tendencies?" Be aware and watch everything that happens at that time. So, you are not doing nothing. Witness whatever is occurring; this is what will increase your awareness. And when you get home, reflect on it. "What did I achieve by getting involved in those things? Why have I come to Earth? Is this what I have come to do?" Contemplate the goal of your life. Ask yourself, "What is my ultimate purpose? How much time do I need to give every day in order to achieve it?"

Then you can decide that if you do indulge in maya, it will be only for a certain period of time and not more than that. If you watch TV, it would be for a decided amount of time and then you will switch it off. Decide about everything and then do it, and do everything with awareness. Those who live without awareness get drawn into the quicksand of maya. They become worse with time and get increasingly entrapped in this maya. If you live with awareness, this will stop happening with you and your alertness will rise.

37
Definite Remedy For Freedom from Thoughts

Whenever I quarrel with my husband or other family members, I cannot control my thoughts. Is there anything I can do to get rid of these thoughts?

You can practice meditation in this situation. It's possible to detach from thoughts during meditation. The mind gets stuck to thoughts and doesn't let go. That is why a lot of meditation techniques have been invented. These techniques help to defocus from negative thoughts. Even a small experiment that you try will work to take your mind off the problem. First, accept that stress has arisen. Then think, "What can be done now? Which meditation can I practice?" Practice any meditation technique* that you have learnt.

Also, it's very important to ask yourself, "*Who* is stressed? *Who* is not being able to divert from these thoughts? Where is the ache, the pain, or strain? Where is the sensation that is troubling me?" Tighten your body and then let it lose, lie down in *shavasana*, and drink some cold water. In this way, you can divert your attention from those thoughts.

Meditation techniques can be learnt from various books on the subject. These techniques will assist you in learning how to meditate on the breath or how to catch various subtle sounds. If you shift your attention from the given incident and focus on anything else, you will come out of anger in some time. But this is a temporary solution.

Later you have to expand your understanding of the truth and arrive at a permanent solution. You have to investigate: "Why does this anger and stress occur? What is the root cause?" Listening, reading, and contemplating the truth will help you to understand the real reason behind the anger and get rid of it permanently. This is the path of Self-enquiry.

By following this path, you will gain the insight that your body is just a mirror, in which you can see your true self—all the time. As you deepen your understanding, you will reach your center or *tejasthan* within, where the Self connects with the body. You may repeatedly forget your true self by getting lost in thoughts and start living in your head. But when you have joined a *satsang*, your attention will be drawn back to the Self. Again and again, you will be reminded to ask: "Who am I? Who gets all these thoughts? Ask this question and reach your center within." On reaching your center, you will experience and remember who you actually are. Thereafter, all thoughts will originate from the center. Gradually, you will get used to living in this manner. Then, for every problem and any decision, you would want to decide by being who you truly are.

In this way, by following the path of Self-enquiry**, you will reach your true self. Then you will get only those thoughts that are necessary.

---

*You can read the book *You Are Meditation* by Sirshree to learn different techniques of meditation.
**Who Am I Now? is the book by Sirshree which elaborates on the process of Self-enquiry, which easily leads you to the Self.

38
Seer, Seen, and Seeing

How does the mind work in the state of *samadhi*? What is the experience like in that state? And how do external incidents help us to remember our true self?

Whenever you sit for *samadhi*, remember that the two obstacles which often arise are the 'checker' and the 'taker.' The 'checker' is an aspect of the mind which always keeps checking whether what is expected to happen in samadhi is happening or not. After this comes the credit 'taker,' another aspect of the mind, which claims, "*I* had this experience." As your understanding of truth grows, the power of both the credit taker and checker begins to diminish. When their strength fades, that's when the state of samadhi intensifies.

It is difficult to experience samadhi when the checker and taker are active. In order to weaken them, whenever the checker within you becomes active, simply smile. You know that it wants to check your present state, but it cannot, because that is beyond its realm. Thus, whenever it emerges, just ignore it. Both the checker and taker are aspects of the mind that hinder the state of samadhi. You will automatically understand the experience of *being* during samadhi; there is absolutely no need for any checker in that state.

During samadhi, the seer, the seen, and seeing become one and make you experience your true self. Let us try to understand this with an example. There is a picture in which a person is looking at a pigeon. So here, the person is the seer, the pigeon is the seen, and what is occurring between them is seeing. But for the one outside this picture, all three are part of the same picture.

Likewise, when you find yourself out of the picture of this illusory world, out of inside and outside of this world, that's when you find your true self. You realize, "I am not the body; I am connected with this body. And it is the body which is seeing the scene. But the one (the real 'I') who is watching all this is separate and out of the picture."

In the state of samadhi, all three (seer, seen, and seeing) become one. The individual or 'seer' in the picture is your body-mind, the 'seen' is whichever object your body-mind is seeing, and the process occurring between them is 'seeing.' The real you—the unlimited formless Self—can see all three as distinct from you and part of one picture. In fact, in the wakeful state too, all that appears in front of you, the very purpose of everything in this world of maya, is for you to remember your true self. All three—seer, seeing, seen—exist only to help you remember yourself. But since you are not aware of this, you lose yourself in the details, in the content of the 'seen.' When the inherent oneness of the seer, seen, and seeing is perceived, you become aware of your true self. And that is the state of samadhi.

Although in the beginning you get entwined in events, but later on you understand that these events have come to assist you, and they are telling you, "Please don't pay attention to us, we are here only to help you." Now this is interesting that someone comes to aid you and asks not to pay attention to them. These incidents are like angels for you. When angels are invisible, people are often unable to take their help; and when they appear visibly, people get caught up in them. This is the reason that human beings don't understand the indications being given by nature in the form of incidents and then complain that these signs should be clearer. But when the signs manifest very clearly, people get caught up in them, because the nature of mind is such that it creates problems in both situations.

Your body-mind is the seer which is seeing a scene/seen. The seer, seen, and seeing are telling you, "Happiness does not lie in us. We cannot help you derive joy from us because you are the one that can create joy within you—the source of joy lies within you. We have come just to convey this to you. So, please don't seek happiness in us." When you finally decipher this hidden message given by events, then there is no problem, and you can be happy in any situation.

Nature is always trying to help you in its invisible form, but you are unable to take advantage of it; so it helps you in a visible form in the guise of events. You have to learn to benefit from them. All this is part of the training to be taken by each one of us on Earth; hence get trained and progress ahead.

SECTION V

Unfolding the Mysteries of Karma

39
Soul of Karma

If I happened to perform a bad karma but the intention behind it was good, then what kind of fruit will it yield?

In order to figure out what fruit it will yield, it is important to understand the *karmatma* behind the action. *Karmatma* means the soul of an action. It comprises of the underlying intention, love, and the understanding behind performing the karma. Many a time, an action may seem wrong from the outside, but the underlying intention is right. The fruit of such action will appear on the basis of the intention, because the motive behind the karma is more important. If an action is being performed with the right intention, love, and right understanding, then it will cause no harm to the giver or receiver.

However, sometimes the intention may be right, but the action lacks wisdom or understanding. For example, parents want their child to do well in life; hence they punish him whenever he commits a mistake to make sure he does not repeat it. But recurrent use of this method gives rise to an inferiority complex within the child, which continues even after growing up. Although the parents' motive is right, which is to make him responsible and independent, they end up harming him because the required understanding is lacking.

Thus, the right intention, understanding, and love, all three are equally important. These three components are the soul of every karma. Without the right understanding, the soul is not complete. If all three factors are present while doing anything, then you need not worry about its fruit at all.

Therefore, before performing any karma, examine and ensure its soul. Once that's ensured, then whatever be the action, it will yield the supreme fruit. And what is the supreme fruit? It is awakening and liberation. This means your karma* with the right soul will lead to the attainment of truth and liberation.

---

*If you wish to attain complete clarity on karma, you can read the book *100% Karma* by Sirshree.

40

Karma and Fruits of Past Lives

One person is born in a poor family, another in a rich family, and yet another is an orphan. On what basis does this occur? Which karma are responsible for this difference?

The principle of karma can be viewed from two points of view. The first is from the viewpoint of an individual, who leads his life assuming himself to be the body. The second is from the viewpoint of the Self.

If seen from the perspective of an individual, then every individual has heard a lot about past lives and past life karma. With these beliefs, all they see when a child is born is whether he is born in poverty or prosperity… whether his family is good or bad… he lived his life… and then he died. They think that every child himself is responsible for his life.

However, the perspective of Self is totally the opposite. When you look at it from the viewpoint of Self, you will understand that man considers himself to be the body and the doer (do-er) of everything, but in reality, he isn't. The Self is the only living entity and the operator of everything. Only after understanding this, it would be clear that it is the Self which is performing all the karma through every body. All the bodies that were ever born up to this day, it is the Self that has performed actions through them and it is the Self that is bearing the fruit of those karmas—be it good fruit or bad. In this way, if you look at things from the perspective of Self, all definitions change. There is a paradigm shift.

Also, the Self always wants to have different experiences through different bodies. Let's understand this using an analogy.

There is an earthen pot and a person puts a hand inside it. There are all kinds of things inside the pot. Since all the fingers are of different sizes, they touch different things in the pot. One finger touches mud and another touches paper. Yet another gets pricked by a needle, while the fourth one feels the soft touch of a cotton ball. In this way, each finger gets a different experience. But the fact is that the person who is actually experiencing everything is out of the pot. All those experiences that the fingers had, turn into memories. The person is still out of the pot. Now based on those experiences and memories, the person puts the other hand in the pot. This is because the finger which got pricked by a needle does not wish to go back into the pot. Hence, the person uses the fingers of the other hand to have further experiences.

The fingers in the pot symbolize all the bodies in the universe and the person outside the pot signifies the Self. Thus, the one who experiences everything through the bodies is none other than the Self. It is the Self that performs all the karma as well as bears all the fruits—whether good or bad. Here if we consider the perspective of an individual (a finger), it thinks, "Look at the experience I had! I don't know what bad karma I'd done to deserve this bitter fruit!"

The Self continues its experiences in further bodies that are born. This game is going on since eons. This is the divine game or *leela* of God. You may know of many children who are extremely talented or knowledgeable right from childhood. For instance, a child may be an exceptional singer or musician at a very young age. This happens because of the past experiences of Self in song and music. The Self uses those experiences and memories in the body of that child. Thus, it is the Self which is gradually propelling itself towards further advancement through that child.

Let us consider another example. In the beginning, people used to live in jungles. Then someone got a thought from the Self, due to which he cut a tree and made a wheel. The wheel brought about a radical increase in the speed of transportation. Similarly, the Self inspired different kinds of inventions by giving thoughts to people, and thereby development continued. The wheel was made by some people, and this experience was taken forward and used by the Self in further bodies to bring about other advanced inventions. This cycle is going on since ages and will continue for ages. But since man is unaware of this game and does not remember that he is the Self and not the body, he has many complaints, such as: "I was born in a poor family, why did this happen with me? This must be due to my past life karma..." and so on.

Instead of thinking in this manner, one should contemplate, "*Who was actually born? Who am I?* Who is operating and expressing through my body?" When the individual understands that all experiences are being experienced by the Self, he will surrender in devotion, and always remain in the feeling of wonder and joy.

41

Karma Associated with Illness

Is getting afflicted by a serious disease due to past life karma or can there be another reason behind it?

Answer for a beginner on the spiritual path:

When you live without much awareness, your actions arise from the tendencies you have developed. It is a misunderstanding that what is happening today in your life is a result of some past life karma. You have carried tendencies and habits within you, not karma. Events occur in your life according to your tendencies. You feel anger, envy, or hatred for others because of these wrong tendencies. As these negative feelings grow, they manifest as disease.

If you pour water on a line drawn on the ground, it flows along that line. Here, it can be said that water develops the tendency of flowing down that line. When an action is repeated multiple times, it becomes a tendency. Its result will be the same in the present as well as in the future.

Thus, actions performed due to old tendencies enhance stupor and ignorance. On the other hand, if you perform actions with awareness, no tendencies will be formed. Awareness is the only way out of negative tendencies—however deep they may be. Developing awareness is the most essential karma. The tendency of living in stupor is bondage. If you are attached to your tendencies even after attaining the knowledge of truth, then these tendencies can draw you away from the truth. You will forget your actual purpose on Earth by getting stuck in your habits.

After attaining knowledge of truth, even if a little bit of stupor remains, then your tendencies will raise their heads once again. Therefore, you need to perform the karma of acquiring the understanding of truth. This will give you clarity about the science of karma, the principles of karma, and the laws of nature. Thereby, you will also be able to gradually bring changes in your mental karma that occur due to ignorance.

When you think negatively about someone, it means you are performing negative mental karma. Although, at the time, you may feel that you did not personally harm anyone and just thought negatively in your mind. However, if the wrong thought is repeated frequently, it can become a tendency. Then the actions that occur due to that tendency reap fruit of those mental karma.

Those, who come to know the laws of karma and act accordingly, are able to attain liberation from bondages of all visible and invisible karma. They are able to lead and enjoy a free life.

The Final Answer of Spirituality:

To begin with, it is imperative to understand the basis on which people say that past life karma is responsible for illness. This is because genes and hereditary factors also play a major role in causing diseases and disorders. If we seek the origin of the family tree of a child, we trace it back to the parents, grandparents, great grandparents, parents of great grandparents… if we continue to go back, we finally reach the Creator of the universe—the Self. It becomes clear that everyone is a part of Self. All births and rebirths are that of the Self. The Self has been taking birth in various bodies. The body-mind doesn't have births or past lives, because only the Self is a living entity. Thus, all actions are that of Self, and the Self alone is bearing the fruit of its own karma through all bodies. It is in this context that some people say that the karma of past lives are the cause of present problems and illnesses. However, if actions are carried out in the present for awakening the Self and realizing our true nature, then it is possible to achieve liberation from the fruit of karma. For example, if a person has a hereditary illness but leads a balanced (*sattvik*) life, then he does not *suffer* from that illness.

Even if the popular opinion about a certain individual is good, no one can gauge that individual's inner state. Often, people seem to be good, but we don't know what is happening inside them. It depends on what kind of thoughts and prayers they are harboring in their life. For example, there is a good person who harbors thoughts like: "I am quite a decent man and always think about the wellbeing of others. But others are so bad, they do such awful things and also behave atrociously with me. Perhaps bad things always happen with good people."

The thought, "Bad things always happen with good people," is also a karma. The person is totally unaware of this. He has no inkling that he has unknowingly performed a negative karma by thinking in this way. This is why people usually don't talk about the karma of the present life and instead keep saying, "This is the result of past life karma." If the topic of present life karma is raised, people come up with reasons and arguments to justify their actions.

Everything that emerges outside originates from one's inner state. If someone is performing some good deeds externally, it means some good mental karma are occurring in their thoughts. Similarly, if one is performing some wrong acts, it means the seeds of those negative actions are hidden somewhere within their thoughts. They are not aware of this because they can only see what is externally visible; that is why they complain that they are good individuals but bad things happen with them.

Again, this is only part of the answer. The complete answer is that the karmas of this life have given an opportunity for past memories to surface. Hence, it's important to decide what new actions the person should perform and what positive prayers and thoughts he or she should cultivate. This is the right step for today.

Now, let us consider what you can practically do when someone is afflicted by a disease. Your presence, your faith, your hope, and your perspective with which you see the issue is of prime importance. Your presence around a sick person should be so positive that they should start feeling that they can get well. Quite often, we look at a patient with pity. This attitude is not at all beneficial for them. Instead, we can try to awaken the Self within them by saying, "You are a part of God, and God cannot be sick. You are free. You are freedom. You *can* get well. Many people have faced such illnesses and totally recovered from them. You are healthy. You are health." Your conviction can change their thoughts. We have to become instrumental in changing people's thoughts. The world today needs positive thoughts.

Most people in the present times have tuned their thoughts towards negativity and unrest. They have to be gently guided back towards peace. Therefore, every morning and night at 9:09, a prayer* is being offered by many people for world peace and global healing. You too can offer this prayer and become part of this transformational initiative. Many other programs are also being conducted with the purpose of transforming people's thought patterns. You too can be

---

*This prayer by Tejgyan is available on YouTube.

a catalyst for this change by participating in those programs and inspiring others to do the same. As a result, if a sick person is able to change his thoughts, then he will spontaneously attract everything that is essential for his health and healing.

If someone's ill-health is affecting your happiness, then start making a conscious effort to increase your level of happiness. Gather information about which branch of medicine or therapy can cure that ailment, and act accordingly. Then watch how your joy helps in solving the problem. If your joy is falling short and you cannot see much positive results, then tell your mind, "Look at the situation from the Self's point of view." In this way, gradually the problem of ill-health will start getting solved.

42

How to Attain Liberation from Bondage of Karma

Whether we perform good karma or bad karma, it leads to bondage. If that's the case, what should we do throughout the day?

Let us understand this dilemma. It is true that bondage of karma is like a pair of handcuffs. Bad deeds result in iron handcuffs and good deeds in gold handcuffs. But both are handcuffs after all. They will bind you. This is why you have to achieve liberation from both kinds of karma. It is not just bad karma that binds you, but good karma leads to ego, which again results in bondage. So, if good karma causes bondage, then is it actually bad karma?

Then what should be done? This is where knowledge comes in. If there is no knowledge of truth, then bad karma is of course bad, but even good karma yields bad fruit. An ignorant person's lie is a lie, but their truth is also a lie.

The good news is that if you can get caught in the bondage of karma, you can also be liberated from it. Let us consider an example to understand how this can be achieved.

When you insert a straw in soap water and blow air in it, bubbles froth up and fill the entire container. When you stop blowing, slowly the bubbles break and a time comes when all of them vanish.

It's the same with our bodies. Soapy water in the form of the mind is present within us; air is being blown in and bubbles are arising. Here 'blowing air' signifies the unconscious repetition of certain behaviors which results in the formation of tendencies or bubbles. If you stop blowing air, new bubbles will automatically stop forming. This means if you consciously stop repeating negative behaviors, new tendencies will stop forming in your mind. As the already formed bubbles rise to the surface and break, all your tendencies will slowly dissolve.

There are some deep tendencies in every human body, which are responsible for repetition of old karma. For example, if someone swears at an individual, he swears back right away. If someone raises a hand to slap him, he immediately raises his hand too. He has this habit right from childhood. This tendency has become fixed. He reacts to every episode in life in the same manner as he reacted the very first time.

An individual follows this mode of conduct during his entire life. A slap is answered with a slap and abuses are answered with abuses. This goes on in unawareness and ignorance. The individual is not even aware that he responds in the same manner every time. This is how bondage of karma is formed. Some new karma are being carried out and some old ones are bearing fruit and dissolving. This vicious cycle is constantly going on.

You have to achieve freedom from this cycle. To do so, you have to "do nothing" the whole day. Here "doing nothing" does not mean the body-mind should do nothing. Let the body-mind engage in its activities; only don't let the sense of doership—the feeling of "I did this"—enter the picture.

When you realize your true self and get permanently established in that state, after that too all the actions will occur through your body-mind, but the feeling of "I did this" will be absent. This means you will be free from the sense of doership. Actions will take place in your (Self's) presence, and you will witness your body carrying out actions. It is only then that "not doing in spite of doing" and "doing in spite of not doing" will be possible for you. This is exactly what Lord Krishna has mentioned in the *Gita*.

You may have seen children playing with a spinning top. Although the top spins at a high speed, it appears as if it's absolutely still. You too have to perform your actions in that manner. It means even while performing actions, you should be able to look at those actions simply like a witness, with the feeling that you are not doing anything. Yet nobody will tell you, "Why aren't you doing anything?" Non-doing is an inner feeling, an inner state.

The sense of doership entangles you in the individual ego. If there is smoke, be it black or white, either way it is smoke and harmful for health. Hence, it has to be got rid of at once. Likewise, you have to get rid of the ego of doership for every action, be it good or bad. If you can be free of this fundamental error of believing yourself to be the doer, you will automatically get the answer to your question. After attaining the understanding of truth, you will find that there is no ego even if the body does a lot of work. The one that is saying "I have done this" has to be eliminated. Spirituality helps you to eliminate it.

43

Good Karma, Bad Karma, and Akarma

Is the journey of karma always from bad karma to good karma, and then from good karma to akarma? Is it right to surrender your bad karma too to God?

First of all, let us clarify that akarma means no-karma or non-doing—i.e. performing actions without the sense of doership because you surrender all your actions to God or Self.

When you begin to surrender your every action to God, a question that arises in your mind is whether you should surrender your mistakes too. The answer is, "Yes, you should." But some people say, "If this is the case, then a person may continue carrying out bad karma and then conveniently surrender them to God. If he adopts this attitude, then his karma will go on binding him."

What you need to realize here is that if you have truly understood and internalized the science of karma, then bad karma will spontaneously stop occurring through you. The question of surrendering bad karma won't even arise.

To begin with, surrender all the wrong karma or mistakes that have occurred through you due to ignorance or unawareness. Then ask yourself, "Have I truly understood karma and its soul (*karmatma*)?" If the answer is yes, then bad karma will automatically stop happening through you. And if the answer is no, then try to understand the topic completely and deeply. Karma which is done with the right understanding can lead you to liberation. This means you will be free from the cycle of life and death of the 'individual ego.' The individual ego is the feeling of apparent separateness from everything, the sense of "I am a separate individual," or the false 'I.' When this ego ceases to exist, every action will occur through the state of akarma or no-karma.

If the intention behind this question is that one wants to continue indulging in bad karma, then they have not understood the definition of karma. To begin with, they will have to understand the difference between karma and reaction. Very often what you think of as karma (action), is in fact, a reaction. This means you gave such a reaction, an automatic reaction, to a situation which you did not want to. In this case, that's not even a karma.

A karma occurs in the space of response, because in that space, you have the freedom of choice. It can be called as the 'Space of Freedom to Choose your Response.' This is the space where you get the chance to think about what kind of response is appropriate for a given situation. That's because you are free from any kind of label in that space. The label may be that of a brother, sister, father, mother, government servant, businessman, employee, or anything else. Thereby, you can be free from all bias in this space. This helps you to think openly and then take the decision of how you want to respond to the situation. This is the place from where you act knowing your true, formless self. This is where karma begins. After that, you have to figure out what is the intention and the ignorance hidden within that karma.

So, first you have to surrender the fruit of the karma to God, with the understanding that this karma has been performed by God through your body. This means you have surrendered or given up the credit of that action. And then if the credit of that action happens to go to someone else, you won't have any objection. As your understanding about the intention, feeling, and understanding (*karmatma*) behind each action increases, the karma occurring through you will reach its heights. You will begin to become one with your true nature, one with God.

44

The Fruit of Bad Karma

If a person is bearing the fruit of his bad karma, then is it only because of his bad karma, or is it that nature is teaching a lesson to his family members by punishing him?

First of all, remove the word 'bad' from the phrase "the fruit of bad karma." Most people believe that if something wrong is happening with them, it must be the fruit of their bad karma. The fact is people have no clue about which karma bears which fruit. Neither do they know whether the punishment someone is going through is really a punishment or a reward.

The reality is that it's the Self which is learning lessons through every fruit of every individual. It's the Self which is going through different experiences. And because of this, it's the story of Self which is progressing in and through every person's life. However, in the entire world, there are very few people who actually contribute to the growth and evolution of this story. The rest waste their time standing in various queues. Some stand in queues outside a movie theater, some outside a club or a restaurant, and some at the doctor's clinic. Such people are only concerned with their bodies. They do not contribute to the progress of the story of Self. Progress is brought about only by those people who are learning life's lessons. It's the Self performing the karma and it's the Self learning the lessons. When you look from the perspective of Self, you will realize how the Self is expressing itself through every body.

For example, a writer-director of a play allots dialogues full of abuses to one actor and only sweet words to another actor. Would you call this as his bad karma or his creativity? It is creativity that enables him to utter different dialogues through different characters. This is not bad karma. Self is doing the same with various bodies. The actions that occur through different people bring about a new scene and take the Self's story forward.

To increase the awareness and understanding of people, some are given punishment and others are given lessons as part of the fruit of karma. Some are learning their lessons by watching someone else's experiences, whereas others go through the fruit of their own karma to learn their lessons.

Mankind thinks it is the story of man which is advancing through all these events. The reality is, all that exists is the Self, all the karma are of Self, and it's the Self which is experiencing the fruit of punishment through one body, and learning lessons by watching this through another body.

45
Freedom from Past Karma

How can we change the prayers that we have done in the past?

Suppose you are very young and bought something from the market. But then for some reason, you need to return it. You may not have the courage to return it to the shopkeeper all by yourself and hence you take an adult along with you.

This happens with many people. This example can help you understand the significance of the Guru's grace. It implies that the prayers you have done can be changed only by the grace of the Guru.

Learn how to become free of any new bondage of karma by applying the knowledge you attain from the Guru. If you can do this, it is possible to get liberated from all bondages of past, present, and future all together, and then perennially remain in the free state. Thereafter, any minor or major upset won't ruffle you, because you would have learnt to remain stable in the state of freedom.

Before you achieve that stability, the state of freedom repeatedly slips away because you frequently operate from the wrong assumption that you are the body. This error occurs because you haven't become totally empty yet. Hence, keep trying to make yourself empty and resolve that, "I will fill only those thoughts within me, which will help me to become empty." Allow only that spark to enter you, which will turn into the fire of wisdom and annihilate all your wrong beliefs in one go. Attain spiritual knowledge and continue positive prayers.

Also, strengthen your new prayers which you are offering with understanding. To do so, offer a prayer that states: "Let my past karma bear fruit in such an easy manner that I tide through it smoothly without even realizing it. Let me happily use the fruit to boost my inner power."

SECTION VI

God, Grace, and Prayer

46

Is God Energy or Vibration?

That which is within all of us, which we call as experience of being or God, is it energy or vibration or something else?

God is that within which all vibrations are occurring, God is beyond inside and outside. Vibration and energy are part of this physical world and are inside it. That which is outside the vibration and energy, is called as God. Initially this is not easy to understand. All that people can understand is that everything is energy and vibration. To understand what's beyond it, you will have to experience the Self.

Suppose there is a bioscope. It's a box-like gadget of the olden days with small peeping-holes. You could peek into the box through those peeping-holes and see images inside the bioscope. Imagine that all the vibration and energy is inside the bioscope, and you are watching it from outside. Depending on the frequency of vibration, you can see either mountains or water or something else. Thus, all you can see from outside the bioscope is the play of vibrations. You know that within the human body is a brain that can sense everything in the form of vibrations. However, the fact is that you are outside that brain, outside that body. That which is outside of 'inside-outside' of this world and inside of 'outside-inside' of this world is called as God.

Let us understand this through another analogy. When a balloon is filled with air and both its ends are tied to each other from within, it looks like an apple, or the universe. By knotting its ends, there is a hole created in the center. When you are in that center, you are neither inside nor outside the balloon.

This can only be experienced, not explained. Ordinary people, scientists, experts, or documentaries can try to explain it only to the extent that they can fathom it. Since it is outside of inside and outside, it can only be understood by experiencing it. Some people may say that space (emptiness) is God, others may say that energy is God, and yet others may say something else. Everyone has described it in different ways. What's important is that if people believe it and are living with that faith, then it's good, because in that way they are preparing to move to the next level of wisdom. By continuing to move ahead in this manner, they can eventually reach the real answer—the limitless Self, the experience of *being*.

The first step for you is to understand the vibrations. Along with this, with the help of your spiritual practice, develop the sensitivity to grasp and feel subtler things. You are being trained to practice meditation so that you don't get entwined in some story of your mind, so that you learn to see things as they are. The mind has a habit of exaggerating everything. You have to be careful about this. Your real objective should be to live your life while abiding in the experience of *being*.

People love to talk and to argue that they know this and they know that, but if you observe their life, it doesn't look like they actually know anything. Their life does not reflect any wisdom; in fact, they go on declining by saying things like, "Everything is an illusion, hence do whatever you feel like doing, it makes no difference." There are many so-called *satsangs* of this kind, where such things are said and people get even more entrapped in wrong activities.

When supreme knowledge dawns in your life, you begin to recognize the experience of *being*. To deepen this recognition, continue with your spiritual practice without getting stuck anywhere.

47
Truth, Soul, and Supreme Soul

If the *Atma* and *Paramatma* are one and the same, why are they given different names?

Ice is nothing but water. But if you use both ice and water at home, do you call ice as ice or do you call it water? Obviously, you call it ice because that makes it convenient to communicate what you are talking about.

Similarly, the *Atma* (soul) and *Paramatma* (the supreme soul), both are the same in essence, but one is connected to the body while the other is separate. That's why you cannot call it by the same name because then it would be difficult to convey the two different states.

The soul is in the state of action and the supreme soul is in the state of rest. When something is not in action, it doesn't become different but can be given a different name. Like, if your child is sleeping, and not playing, he is still your child; but when he is playing, he is called a player or sportsman. You say, "My son is a sportsman." When the same child is asleep at night, you say, "My *child* is sleeping." Thus, different words are used for different states, so that everybody understands exactly what one is talking about. Likewise, it is only for ease of communication that God is called as the Atma or Paramatma, although both refer to the same essence.

48

Every Prayer Has a Role

Earlier, when I used to pray, I would chant the names of all the Gods. Now I pray for Self-realization, I pray for getting stabilized in the triad of truth (listening to truth, devotion for truth, and service of truth). Am I moving in the right direction?

You are definitely moving in the right direction. Your current prayers indicate that you have now become capable of receiving the truth.

In the beginning, everyone is given something to repeat or chant, because most people are unable to focus or sit still in one place. This is the reason that people are given some activity to increase their concentration and capacity. This is the objective of most of the rituals and practices which were created since the ancient times. You followed a practice and reaped its benefit; hence the next phase has appeared in your life.

But quite often people get stuck in the thought: "Why my earlier prayer has stopped?" What you need to understand here is that your earlier prayer has played an important role in bringing you to this present state. Now gradually you are moving towards silence. Some old activities fade away because their role is done. Some new activities will begin because their role is commencing in your life. There is nothing wrong with this. Everything is contributing to your spiritual growth.

For example, you burnt some wood to cook some rice. After the rice is cooked, you are not supposed to lament that the wood is gone; instead you need to eat the rice, because it will nourish you.

Thus, you don't need to harbor any kind of fear, because you are now becoming worthy of receiving the truth. Without keeping any doubts in your mind, try to acquire complete understanding of the truth. All those to whom you prayed earlier will be genuinely happy to see you progressing on the spiritual path. All the gurus you have had would want you to progress. Nobody is going to be upset with your state; in fact, they will be satisfied.

The seekers who lack understanding may harbor fears like, "Oh, I have stopped the prayer that this guru had given me; I hope he doesn't get upset with me!" The fact is that whoever is worthy and capable does not get upset. Now you should become incapable of sorrow. Be capable for everything else. If you truly understand this, you will say, there is so much joy in life that there isn't any space for sorrow. Then you can remain happy anywhere in the world.

The prayer for staying in the triad of truth helps every devotee to progress on the path of truth; therefore continue to offer this prayer regularly.

49
Experience Constant Grace

What should I do so that God's grace showers constantly on me?

To experience God's grace constantly, you have to continuously remind yourself of that grace. Always keep a watch to see whether the window of your heart is open or not, so that the showers of grace can come in. It is important to identify and remove the obstacles to that which you want incessantly. To do so, observe and note those situations that reduce your awareness. Only then, you can maintain awareness in those situations.

For example, a person is going for a party. He is aware that he could lose himself (forget his true self) in the party. So, before going, he rubs a little balm for colds on his nose, so that it will keep burning. That sensation will serve as a constant reminder of his true self during the party. You too need such reminders. You have to make some effort for what you want to remember constantly. You have to make some arrangements for things that make you forget your true nature and divine grace. In fact, convert those things that make you forget into reminders.

For instance, if a certain person makes you forget the important spiritual teachings that you would like to remember, gift them special clothes for each day, which will act as reminders for you whenever you see them. This will serve two objectives: they will be happy to receive the gift and you will get your reminder. This was an example of how you can use creative methods for remembering.

In fact, everyone should examine their life and try to find out through contemplation: "How can I make a ladder out of the factors that push me down?" Sometimes a movie can remind you of the truth and sometimes listening to someone. That is why your Guru gives you numerous examples about what all can remind you of truth. Make reminders out of things that make you forget. Film songs can make you forget the truth, but devotional songs created on the same tune can remind you of truth. You will have to learn this art bit by bit, because your desire is for endless grace.

You want grace to always shower upon you and your love for grace to never fade. You need to have an intense love for truth for this to happen. Sometimes, when we get a little relief from our problems, we feel relaxed and think that we don't need to remember anything anymore. But it is essential to have infinite love for truth in order to constantly remember that you have to joyfully take full advantage of whatever time you have on Earth. You don't need to go and sit in a cave for spiritual practice or become so serious that you lose all contact with the world.

Gradually, a time will come when you will say, "All the rubbish inside me has cleared to such an extent that it is now much easier to remember the truth and maintain awareness." It will be difficult initially, but later it will become a beloved effort. Then you will begin to feel God's grace in everything you do. Grace is in fact ever flowing, you only need to recognize it. Enhance your awareness of it and start receiving it.

50
The Necessity of Slow People

I have a friend who speaks very slowly. I feel like shaking her and telling her to speak quickly. While passing through a narrow passage, when the one in front of me is too slow, I get irritated, and this creates problems. How should I deal with this?

You can take two actions. First, sow the seeds for the future about what kind of people you want in your life. You can pray, "I want to be with fast people." You have to communicate your needs very clearly to nature. This is because everything in your life at present is according to your past orders.

Secondly, till these people from your past orders are with you and nature is searching for the people you want in the future, in the meantime you have the opportunity to be creative. Till then, you can look at these slower people as a mirror to show you your reality, and to understand how your presence is affecting the situation. If the other person is slow and you cannot bear it, this means that you lack patience. There are some individuals who are praying for very patient people to come into their lives. These are the same people for whom you are praying that they should become faster. As a result, faster people are not appearing in your life and patient people are not appearing in their lives. Both are stuck. If you can tweak your wish a bit, both of you will get your wishes fulfilled. So, what you need to do is, whenever a person is moving slowly in front of you, tell yourself, "I have to increase my patience." That slow person can remind you of a tortoise, and thereby the story of the hare and the tortoise. You can get rid of the mistake the hare had made from your life.

This is also an opportunity to tap into your creativity. Suppose, you have to go out with someone who is taking a long time to get ready. You can either crib and nag, or you can do something creative. You can decide, "I am going to quickly compose a devotional song." Really creative songs can be composed in this manner.

On the other hand, if it is important to reach someplace on time, think of creative ways in which you can ensure they are ready on time. Like you can remind them a day earlier, "We have to reach by 6 pm; be ready." They may ask, "The program is tomorrow; why are you saying this today?" You can say, "So that you are ready on time." In this way, you can enjoy talking with them. Otherwise, if you speak to them in frustration, they would comment something, which in turn would annoy you even more.

Thus, you have to think of various creative ways in which you can remain happy in this situation. If the other person is slow, your creativity should be faster. When you are able to do this, all the slow people in your life will contribute immensely to your growth; you will progress faster due to them. Then a day will come when you will say, "There *should* be some slow people in life, and they should remain in our life until the speed of our creativity increases."

51
Everything Has Already Happened

Sometimes, when an incident is taking place, I feel that this has happened before, although it hasn't. What could be the reason behind this?

Firstly, you should know that this is not very unusual; it happens with a lot of people, not just you. Secondly, consider it as a gift from nature. The fact is, nature gives different gifts to different people. This means it gives those kinds of experiences that will activate people to start seeking the truth.

Nature or God—or whatever name you want to give—is so very creative that it keeps creating things in new ways. When people feel that the event they are witnessing has occurred before, they get shaken and thereby get ready to contemplate. Contemplation leads them to the quest for the final truth. In this quest, they make some discoveries that propel them forward in the journey. Then gradually, all the secrets of nature begin to unfold before them, like how the divine game of this world is going on, how the laws of nature are operating the entire universe, how this incredible game of life has been created, how people are being prepared for the truth by giving them some extraordinary experiences…

There are many things that keep happening with you, and you have no clue why they happen. Like, why were you born into this particular family? Why have these specific events occurred in your life? Why does it feel that everything has already happened before? The reality is that when God wants to realize Himself/Herself, then God begins to work in different ways on different people. One of the ways it begins is the one which is occurring with you. Due to this starting push, many people begin to tread the path of truth, till they reach the final destination. Let's use an analogy to understand this.

There is a temple far away from a village, and the goal of the villagers is to reach this temple. Some people are seen travelling on different paths towards the temple. One person goes to a shop, buys some items, and then proceeds towards the temple. Another person walks directly from his home towards the temple. Yet another goes to school first, studies, meets his parents, and then proceeds towards the temple. So, the fact is that ultimately everyone has to reach the temple, but it seems as if one is going to the temple, another is going to a shop, and the other to school. The exact same thing is happening in real life; everyone is moving towards the same destination but through different routes.

Although, it can happen that the one going directly goes straight to the temple, whereas the one going to school gets diverted, goes somewhere else, and later on comes back on track. This is like when people forget the actual purpose of coming to Earth and fall into bad habits, such as ragging others, gambling, drinking, etc. The point is, the more detours one takes, the more time it will take to reach the destination.

Some people are given the thought "Who am I?" to help them begin the journey towards truth, while some look into a mirror and wonder, "Is this really who I am?" All these are simply different thoughts that appear, so as to lead them to the same goal. In the same way, certain things are happening with you, which are creating curiosity within you. These will become instrumental in turning you towards the truth. This is nature's way of guiding you towards the actual purpose of your life on Earth. Someone may get a dream of the truth; after which they desire to experience the same in reality. In this way, a dream becomes instrumental for some, while it could be a question for others, and for yet some others, it could be a feeling. The purpose of all these is to help everyone reach the supreme truth.

The temple is just an example, it could be a church, mosque, *gurudwara*, or anything else you believe in. The ultimate purpose of all the people on Earth is that God (Self) should be able to express Itself in the highest manner through their human body. However, there is a possibility that some people may stoop lower than animals in this earthly life. This possibility or risk should be eliminated; then we can proceed towards the supreme goal.

Use every event in your life as a stepping stone towards your ultimate destination. At the same time, consider every incident as nature's gift for you, learn from it, and move ahead.

52
Freedom from Old Memories

How can we attain freedom from old memories?

It is possible to flush out old memories from your mind and heart. In fact, it is quite easy to be free from them, but the question is, do you really want that freedom? Let's understand this with the help of an example.

A young boy finds an earthworm in the rain. He wraps it up in a piece of paper and runs home. He then excitedly calls his little brother. "Look, I have brought something in this packet. It's magic!" Now the little brother is curious. "Show me quickly. I want to see what's the magic!"

The boy opens the packet, in which the poor worm is all curled up. He gets a straw and blows air on the worm. The worm feels cold and wriggles a bit. The little brother is delighted. "Wow! That's magic!"

The boy shows this magic to many of his friends. Two days pass in this manner. Eventually, the worm becomes unresponsive because of lack of oxygen in the packet. The next time, when the kid is trying to show his "magic" to someone, the worm does not move. He says, "No problem, it will move next time," and again closes the packet. The worm dies after some time but the kid does not realize this. He repeatedly tries to make it move, but you know that's not going to happen.

Human nature is similar. The past is not bad, it is dead. This means old memories are not bad, but they are dead. People simply don't accept this. They too have a straw—the straw of thoughts—through which they keep blowing on past memories. When thoughts are blown on past memories, they come alive. The worm of past memories eventually dies but people keep trying to revive it, thinking it must be asleep. They feel, "Let me open the packet of old memories and check, it might give me some joy." They start imagining, "I will open the old packet, I will blow air on it, the worm will move again, I will show it to others, they will praise me…" If these people are successful in this attempt, it will encourage them to keep going back to their past memories.

The needle touches the gramophone record and an old song begins to play. Likewise, some people keep the needle of their attention on their past record, and relive their past memories again and again in their mind. As a result, only that old tune continues to play in their life. It's crucial for them to see this and realize this, in order to get rid of this habit. Those who cannot see it continue to dig into their old memories.

The present is the truth because only the present can give you what you are praying for. You can get something from that which is living, while that which is dead cannot give you anything. As mentioned, the past is not bad, it is dead. Hence, there is no need to indulge in past memories.

With this understanding, you will be able to live with the feeling of freedom.

53

Old Memories and the Next Birth

There was a program on Discovery channel in which a child remembered the house of his previous birth. How is it possible for a child to remember such old memories and that too from his previous birth?

The body by itself is lifeless, it comes alive only when the Self connects with it. From this perspective, all memories belong to the Self; the body has no memories.

The Self undergoes various experiences through different bodies, and the memories of those experiences get collected in the Akashic Records. The Self then re-uses some of those memories by implanting them in a new body. And when these memories get activated, such astonishing cases come to light. Sometimes, one person's memories exist in two or three different people. You may have heard that two or three people are claiming to be the same person in their previous life. This happens when one individual's memories have been implanted in two or three bodies. All these memories are used by the Self in different bodies.

Before asking a question on this topic, it is essential to carry out deep and thorough research on questions such as, what were the kind of cases on this topic and how many of them have been proven to be authentic. Ultimately, the truth is, it is memories that are re-used in human bodies. The ego or the sense of separateness, which is attached to these memories, gives rise to the belief that, "I am separate. I am a separate individual. These are *my* memories."

Let us understand these memories with another example. When you are seeing a dream, you are convinced that everything is actually happening with you, but when you wake up, you know that it was just an imagination. The implanted memories also have the same effect as a dream; the person feels that this has definitely happened with them at some time or the other. On gaining knowledge of the Self, the dream ends and the person realizes that it was just an illusion, nothing has happened with them.

The reality is, the Self keeps the old memories going in different bodies. Those who are not aware of this game of Self, are bound to believe in rebirth of a particular individual. But that's not true.

54

Rebirth of the Astral Body

I am aware that there is rebirth of Consciousness or Self, but does the astral body also get reborn with it?

First of all, let's understand that apart from the Self, everything else is lifeless. Only the Self is the living entity, which gives life to anything it permeates. If this process has to be described in words, it can be called as "rebirth" of Self. However, this word is also wrong, because how can that which never dies be reborn? Actually, the external sheath or shell falls off and is recreated, again and again. This means all the physical bodies degenerate and disintegrate, and new bodies are created all the time.

The astral body is also basically a sheath or covering, although on a subtle level. The astral body is more potent than the physical body, but this does not mean that the astral body can be reborn, because the only living element is the Self. Everything else is like bricks, stones, and cement, which is the raw material used for new construction. If the rubble from a building that has broken down, is used in ten new buildings, it doesn't mean that the previous building is reborn ten times. Only its material has been reused. From the perspective of the Self, this material means the body, thoughts of the mind, and memories of experiences. All the thoughts, memories, and experiences of all the beings that have ever lived are automatically stored in the universal memory bank known as Akashic Records. Then the important experiences of bodies, which were scientists, doctors, artists, etc. are reused in new bodies to bring about a new scene and advancement in the universe. In this way, a platform is made available for new bodies to take the world further. Another purpose of implanting old memories in new bodies is to heal the painful memories* that are present in the Self's memory bank.

However, when the old memories are implanted in new bodies, it often leads to misunderstanding in the new bodies that "I was this particular person in my last birth." The fact is, no person is ever reborn. The Self, through its automatic system, keeps using past memories and experiences in new bodies. If we need to give some words to this process, we can say that the Self is reborn.

The astral body is not reborn; only its memories are used. The astral body's journey continues for thousands of years, so its memories can be used at any time. All this is available in the Akashic Records. Just like in a record store, there are countless records, CD's, DVD's, and every year the shopkeeper takes out some of them to take a look at them, similarly the Self uses memories. These memories are reborn and not the astral body.

---

*You can read more on this subject in an upcoming book on Life Lessons and the Healing of Painful Memories, authored by Sirshree.

SECTION VII

Living According To The Divine Plan

55

All Possibilities Are Pre-decided

Is it true that my every action, reaction, thought, and circumstance is pre-decided?

People tend to misunderstand the term 'pre-decided' or 'predestined.' If someone is a thief, people think it was pre-decided that he will be a thief. But the fact is, it is also pre-decided that he can become anything else that he chooses to—he can become a monk, or someone like Sage Valmiki, or the dacoit Ratnakar. All options are available for him. This means that all the possibilities of a person are pre-decided or predestined. What's important is which option a person chooses, what does he click on.

Suppose there is a website. As soon as you open it, many options appear before you, such as: physical, mental, financial, spiritual, etc. Depending on what you want, you click on one option and it opens. On that page, you find something else and you go deeper by clicking on it. It also opens and you find one more option on it and you proceed to click on it. Then you may decide that you don't want to go further in that direction. So, by clicking on 'home,' you can get back to where you started.

In the exact same way, in life, it is important which option you click on. Both possibilities are simultaneously available: there is the possibility of a happy life and also that of a miserable life. The aim of spirituality is to teach the art of clicking on the right option.

People who believe in destiny take the opposite meaning. They believe, "This is what is going to occur in my life; nothing else can happen." In this way, by repeatedly thinking of what they feel is destined for them, they attract it into their life. For example, if a thief believes that his life is going to end as a thief in a prison, he repeats this thought subconsciously and attracts that end to his life. That's why efforts are made to increase people's knowledge, so that they can click on newer and higher possibilities for themselves.

It is the Self that presents all the possibilities before you—through someone or something. Like, you get the news through someone, "You can listen to a discourse now," and you get one more news through someone else, "Let's go to this restaurant." Now the decision you make will depend upon the kind of choices you have been making till date. You may not make the right choice at present. It is only when you gain the knowledge and understanding of truth that you will choose the right option.

People always make choices according to their understanding. Animals, on the other hand, have no choice but to do what nature makes them do. That is why, their entire life from birth to death is under nature's control. But human beings have all options open before them. This is the reason that humans have limitless possibilities.

For instance, there are many people who listen to discourses and come to know the truth. But it depends on each one's understanding whether they can pay attention to that which helps them in making the right choices and applying that wisdom in their everyday life.

Thus, all possibilities are predestined or pre-decided. What you choose depends upon your decisions, which in turn are based upon the level of your awareness and understanding.

56

The Journey from Feelings to Action

My feelings, thoughts, and words are aligned with each other most of the times, but not my actions. How can I align my actions?

Everything happens first at the level of feelings, then thoughts, followed by speech, and then actions. When you listen to the truth, you feel a change first at the level of feeling. You experience a difference in your feelings, and slowly your feelings become the same as the feelings of Self—they become one.

When a father wants his son to do something, and if the son does it, the father feels happy. In this way, the joy of the father and the son becomes the same, becomes one. This helps the son to know that he is proceeding in the right direction.

We always understand through feelings whether we have taken the right path or not. But the job is not yet done, because then the thoughts corresponding to the feelings begin to arise. We get more thoughts about whatever we give importance to. This process is such that first the feeling from the Self conveys that you are on the right track, then thoughts about it start appearing, then it comes in your speech, and finally in your actions. Action is the last step.

Let's reconsider the example of overflowing water. The tap in the bathroom is running and the bucket is filling with water. After the bucket is full, the water starts overflowing. This can be regarded as the water coming into action. Then the water flows out into the room, the hall, spreads into the neighborhood, and also reaches your office. In other words, the effect of the truth that you have attained is first seen by your family members, then your neighbors, and then your colleagues. Thus, among your feelings, thoughts, words, and actions, it's your actions that show their effect everywhere.

If your feelings, thoughts, words, and actions are not happening in this order, then first of all stop judging this as something wrong. Then reflect upon whether you are shutting off the tap while the bucket is filling. In other words, are you suppressing your feelings? If feelings have been stopped, the process cannot proceed further.

Every night before sleep, recollect all your activities throughout the day, and ask yourself, "During which action did I feel hampered? Which action was I supposed to carry out, but couldn't? At that time, what had I forgotten? What did I give importance to during that time, and instead what should I give importance to the next time? Do I still harbor the fear of losing something? Do I still have some greed, which I want to fulfill through others? Which internal vice or flaw is still within me, which is preventing me from coming into action?" Asking yourself these questions will prove to be helpful. These questions will align your actions with your feelings, thoughts, and words.

Suppose, your feeling is conveying that you are on the right track, and the feeling of the Self is the same as your feeling. In spite of this, if you are not feeling good during the action, then it means some more inner work needs to be done in this area.

The good news is, you know that you have to work in this area. Therefore, ask yourself, "How can I take the required step to work on this?" The next day, be aware and proceed towards taking that step. In this way, gradually your actions will become aligned.

Whenever you experience a 100% conviction, then that feeling manifests into action. If conviction is lacking even in the slightest, then the process stops at the level of speech. Hence, work on deepening your conviction on the truth. To do so, you need to listen to the truth, read books on the truth, contemplate the truth, and be in the right company. Spend your maximum time with people who have 100% conviction on the truth. At the same time, keep a watch over what kind of fears keep arising in you. If you continue to do this persistently, then the truth that has come in your feelings, thoughts, and words, will definitely come into your actions too.

57

The Divine Plan

From the highest perspective, what is the meaning of the Divine Plan?

The best performance of the Self while connected to the body is the Divine Plan. According to the divine plan, everything is in abundance, but humans don't know how to make use of it. You may have heard people asking, "Is it true that I will get only what is written in my destiny and not anything else?" Such people are told, "First you should be able to *receive* what is in your destiny." Because the fact is, there is such abundance in everyone's destiny, that this lifespan will fall short to fully receive everything. This is why, first you need to pray, "I should be able to fully receive all that is written in my destiny."

But most people keep agonizing over the thought, "Is this thing in my destiny or not?" Such thoughts prevent you from receiving everything that is available for you. This type of thinking acts as an obstacle in the path of those things that are waiting to come to you. This knowledge and training is being given to you, so that you stop creating those obstacles.

What is known as 'destiny' in the world, is called as the 'divine plan' at the spiritual level. When people don't get something they want, they blame and complain about their fate. But if they think in terms of the divine plan, they become more accepting. Even if they haven't got what they wanted, yet they feel good by thinking, "I will get what is in my divine plan. And what is not in my divine plan, I don't even want it." Everyone gets everything abundantly according to their divine plan.

58
Conviction of Truth and Limitless Thinking

How can we increase our conviction on truth? Will my thoughts automatically become limitless after Self-realization?

Having conviction on truth means clearly seeing the truth. This conviction cannot be brought by thinking on it.

Suppose, you have a television and you know that a lot of informative programs can be watched on it, and you can know about the entire world sitting at home. Now imagine there are some people who have no idea about the function of a television and are using the TV-top just for keeping their towels and socks warm in winter.

You would tell them, "Come on, this television can do much more than act like a warmer for your towels and socks."

They may ask, "How do you have so much conviction?"

You would say, "Because I can clearly see that you have reduced the brightness, color, contrast, and sound of the TV to zero. You have only switched the power button on, which is why the TV is radiating some heat, and you are using it for warming your towels."

One who attains Self-realization is called a seer or mystic, because the entire mystery is solved for him, which others cannot even see. This happens because he is looking at possibilities. He can see that if only people would increase the brightness, color, and volume of the television and select the right channel, a lot can happen. In the beginning, people may find this hard to believe and say, "How is it possible that a box can do all this? How can you say this or think like this?" This is because they believe that, like them, others also must be saying things or doing things by thinking and re-thinking. Then the Self-realized one will say, "There's nothing to think about it, because I can see everything crystal clear." The one who is Self-realized simply says what he sees, and for this he doesn't need to think or prepare what to say. He just has to describe what he can clearly see.

When you think of thinking limitless thoughts, you are still thinking within a boundary. As you go on progressing on the path of truth, you realize that your earlier thinking was so very limited. In spite of this, you may find it difficult to fully think and comprehend the Self-realized state, and intermittently slip back to identifying with the body.

If someone works even part-time to attain Self-realization, a lot can happen. Because if you listen to the Self even part-time, a lot of changes begin in your body-mind. When you listen only to the Self at all times, this state is called as Self-stabilization. After you are stabilized in the Self, when someone asks you about the Self, the truth, or this state, you describe whatever you see. Then there is no need to think about it.

59
The Self-expression That Benefits Everyone

How can the Self-expression of truth benefit others? If lethargy hampers this expression, how can we get rid of it?

Sometimes, some people hear some words and are inspired to write a song, a poem, or a hymn. They feel immense joy in writing it. But later, they forget these songs or poems. Such people are advised that although it's good to derive joy from your writing, it would be better if you can use it for the benefit of others too. Whatever comes out straight from the heart should benefit as many people as possible. If a solution for an illness arises from your *tejasthan*, but you forget about it after some time, it means you are being irresponsible. Because if something is coming from within you, it is your responsibility to take it to the world.

In the olden days, it was for this reason that seekers were first trained to render service for five to six years; and during this time, there would be no talk of knowledge. They were made to work hard, so that their bodies became strong and lethargy would not impede their Self-expression after receiving knowledge.

Whenever a hymn emerges from your *being*, first the feeling for it arises, then a thought, then words, then it is written, and finally it is sung or published. Writing has been added to the process, because generally people don't have the habit of writing. Just because of the lack of this habit, very often the Self does not get the opportunity to express itself to the world. Suppose, something is coming from the Self through an individual's body. But if that individual has laziness, the habit of procrastination, as well as lack of communication skills and commitment, then Self-expression cannot occur. Train yourself and learn these skills so that these shortcomings do not hinder your Self-expression.

There are two types of people in this world. The first type are those who have the skill to build something like the Taj Mahal. The second type are those who have the knowledge and experience of how to build a Taj Mahal, and also how it can become a medium for leading people to the path of truth. It is only when both these types of people come together that something like a Taj Mahal can get created. That's why, those who have skills should acquire knowledge and those who have the knowledge should acquire skills. If this happens, then work can be accomplished in the fastest and best manner. Also, this kind of work can benefit everyone.

Using your love and devotion for truth, you can eliminate the lethargy within you. This is the role of devotion, because it is due to devotion that an individual can make his body work. Otherwise, it is more likely that he becomes merely a so-called intellectual or knowledgeable loud-mouth.

You have to ask yourself the question: "Would the kind of Self-expression that I am thinking about, benefit others or just myself? What skills or qualities am I cultivating in this body?" It is only through love and devotion that you can express yourself in a way which would benefit all. Let love operate even when the ego arises. Great work and enormous tasks are possible with love and devotion. To enhance your devotion, you can read books on the subject* and listen to discourses. Gradually, your body will get rid of indolence and you will become fully ready for Self-expression.

Essence of Devotion and *100% Devotion* are books by Sirshree on devotion.

60

Living an Impersonal Life

How can we live an impersonal life?

When an individual wants to work on his personal life, then personal management happens, which means the individual manages various aspects of himself in his own way. For instance, if a problem appears, he may use some deception or lies, and try to get rid of the problem by any means. People use whatever methods they have seen or heard all their life to deal with their problems.

Then comes a time when impersonal life begins. At this stage, impersonal work has to be done with understanding of truth. In this process, you learn to solve problems from the highest perspective. Thereafter, even while facing personal problems, you handle them from the highest perspective, from an impersonal standpoint.

When you have the highest viewpoint, you respond to situations and take decisions being who you truly are, even if those situations or decisions are regarding trivial, routine activities like sleeping and eating. You can turn even these into impersonal activities by asking yourself, "Who am I and why am I going to eat? Why am I going to sleep?" With each and every decision, you have to take care of your body, so that the best expression of the Self can take place through it. This is the reason you would do everything, and not because you are the body. Earlier you had been living with the assumption that you are the body. But when you were explained and proved in many ways that you are not the body, then you contemplated it and were convinced about it.

Always remember the understanding of truth that you have gained, and then witness it working in your daily life. Look at yourself taking every decision from the highest perspective. Although, in the beginning, you may not be able to take all decisions in this manner. At that time, you can decide, "If I have to make 100 small or big decisions each day, I will take at least 10 decisions from the highest perspective." Gradually, the number will go on increasing till it reaches a hundred. In this way, by the next year, you will be taking all your decisions from the supreme state—from the Self. This will be possible only when you know and remember the Self before taking decisions. To reach this state, begin with small experiments. This way, you will embark on an impersonal life—a life for others, because there is no other. And only an impersonal life can give you the highest level of happiness.

You can send your opinion or feedback on this book to:
Tej Gyan Foundation, P.O. Box 25, Pimpri Colony,
Pimpri, Pune – 411017, Maharashtra, INDIA.
Email: englishbooks@tejgyan.org

Write for Us

We welcome writers, translators, and editors to join our team. If you would like to volunteer, please email us at: englishbooks@tejgyan.org or call : +91 90110 10963

Appendix

About Sirshree

Sirshree's spiritual quest, which began during his childhood, led him on a journey through various schools of thought and prevalent meditation practices. His overpowering desire to attain the truth made him relinquish his teaching profession. After a long period of contemplation on the truth of life, his spiritual quest culminated in the attainment of the ultimate truth. Since then, over the last two decades, he has dedicated his life toward elevating mass consciousness and making spiritual pursuit simple and accessible to all.

Sirshree espouses, **"All paths that lead to the truth begin differently, but culminate at the same point – understanding. Understanding of truth is complete in itself. Listening to this understanding is enough to attain the truth."**

Sirshree has delivered more than 3000 discourses that throw light on this understanding, simplify various aspects of life, and reveal missing links in spirituality. He delivers the understanding in casual and contemporary language by weaving profound aspects into analogies, parables, and humor that provoke one to contemplate.

To make it possible for people from all walks of life to directly experience this understanding, Sirshree has designed the *Maha Aasmani Param Gyan Shivir* – a retreat designed as a comprehensive system for imparting wisdom. This system for wisdom, which has been accredited with ISO 9001:2015 certification, has inspired thousands of seekers from all walks of life to progress on their journey of the truth. This system makes the wisdom accessible to every human being, regardless of religion, caste, social strata, country, or belief system.

Sirshree is the founder of Tej Gyan Foundation, a no-profit organization committed to raising mass consciousness with branches in India, the United States, Europe and Asia-Pacific. Sirshree's retreats have transformed the lives of thousands and his teachings have inspired various social initiatives for raising global consciousness.

His published work includes more than 100 books, some of which have been translated in more than 10 languages and published by leading publishers. Sirshree's books provide profound and practical reading on existential subjects like emotional maturity, harmony in relationships, developing self-belief, overcoming stress and anxiety, and dealing with the question of life beyond death, to name a few. His literature on core spirituality expounds the deeper meaning of self-realization and self-stabilization, revealing missing links in the understanding of karma, wisdom, devotion, meditation, and consciousness.

Various luminaries and celebrities like His Holiness the Dalai Lama, publishers Mr. Reid Tracy and Ms. Tami Simon, and Yoga Master Dr. B. K. S. Iyengar have released Sirshree's books and lauded his work. *The Source* book series, authored by Sirshree, has sold over 10 million copies in five years. His book *The Warrior's Mirror*, published by Penguin, was featured in the Limca Book of Records for being released on the same day in 11 languages.

Tejgyan... The Road Ahead
What is Tejgyan?

Tejgyan is the wisdom of the existential truth, which is beyond duality. "Gyan" is a term commonly used for "knowledge." Tejgyan is the wisdom beyond knowledge and ignorance. It is the understanding that arises from direct experience of the supreme truth. It is what sets us free from the limitations of the mind and opens us to our highest potential.

In today's world, there are people who feel disharmony and are desperately trying to achieve balance in an unpredictable life. Tejgyan helps them in harmonizing with their true nature, which is the formless and limitless Self, thereby restoring balance in all aspects of their lives.

And then, there are those who are successful, but feel a sense of emptiness within. Tejgyan provides them fulfilment and helps them to embark on a journey towards Self-realization. There are others who feel lost and are seeking the meaning of life. Tejgyan helps them to realize the true purpose of human life.

All this is possible with Tejgyan due to a very simple reason. The experience of the ultimate truth (God or Pure Consciousness) is always available. The direct experience of this truth is possible provided the right method is known. Tejgyan is that method, that understanding.

The understanding of Tejgyan makes it possible to lead a life of freedom from fear, worry, anger, and stress. It helps in attaining physical vitality, emotional strength and stability, harmony in relationships, financial freedom, and spiritual progress.

At Tej Gyan Foundation, Sirshree imparts this understanding through a System for Wisdom – a series of retreats that guides participants step by step to realize the true self, to get established in the experience of self-realization, and to express its divine qualities. This system for wisdom has been accredited with the ISO 9001:2015 certification.

Maha Aasmani Param Gyan Shivir

Maha Aasmani Param Gyan Shivir is the flagship Self-realization retreat offered by Tej Gyan Foundation. The retreat is conducted in Hindi. The teachings of the retreat are non-denominational (secular).

This residential retreat is held for 3-5 days at the foundation's MaNaN Ashram amidst the glory of the mountains and pristine beauty of nature. The Ashram is located at the outskirts of the city of Pune in India, and is well connected by air, road, and rail. The retreat is also held at other centers of Tej Gyan Foundation across the world.

You can participate in this retreat to attain ageless wisdom through a unique System for Wisdom, so that you can:

1. Discover "Who am I?" through direct experience.
2. Learn to abide in pure consciousness while functioning in the world, allowing the qualities of consciousness like peace, love, joy, compassion, abundance, and creativity to manifest.
3. Acquire simple tools to use in everyday life, which help quiet the chattering mind.
4. Get practical techniques to stay in the present and connect to the source of all answers within (the inner guru).
5. Discover missing links in the practices of meditation (*dhyan*), action (*karma*), wisdom (*gyan*), and devotion (*bhakti*).
6. Understand the nature of your body-mind to attain freedom from its tendencies.
7. Learn practical methods to shift from mind-centered living to consciousness-centered living.

A Mini-retreat is also conducted, especially for teenagers (14-16 years of age) during summer and winter vacations.

To register for retreats, visit www.tejgyan.org

Contact (+91) 9921008060, or email mail@tejgyan.com

About Tej Gyan Foundation

Tej Gyan Foundation (TGF) was established with the mission of creating a highly evolved society through all-round development of every individual that transforms all the facets of their lives. It is a non-profit organization, founded on the teachings of Sirshree.

The Foundation has received the ISO certification (ISO 9001:2015) for its system of imparting wisdom. It has centers all across India as well as in other countries. The motto of Tej Gyan Foundation is 'Happy Thoughts.'

At the core of the philosophy of Tejgyan is the 'Power of Acceptance.' Acceptance has profound meaning and is at the core of our *being*. It is acceptance that brings forth true love, joy, and peace in our life.

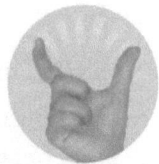

Symbol of Acceptance

The Symbol of Acceptance (shown above) is a representation of this truth. The symbol represents a bracket. Whatever occurs in life falls within this bracket that signifies acceptance of whatever *is*. Hence, this symbol forms the centerpiece of the Foundation's MaNaN Ashram.

The Foundation is creating a highly evolved society through:

- Tejgyan Programs (Retreats, YouTube Webcasts)
- Tejgyan Books and Apps
- Tejgyan Projects (Value education, Women empowerment, Peace initiatives)

The Foundation undertakes projects to elevate the level of consciousness among students, youth, women, senior citizens, teachers, doctors, leaders, professionals, corporate and Government organizations, police force, prisoners, etc.

Now you can register online for the following retreats

Maha Aasmani Param Gyan Shivir
(5 Days Residential Retreat in Hindi)

Mini Maha Aasmani Shivir
3 Days (Residential) Retreat for Teens

🔍 www.tejgyan.org

Books can be delivered at your doorstep by registered post or courier. You can request the same through postal money order or pay by VPP. Please send the money order to either of the following two addresses:

WOW Publishings Pvt. Ltd.

1. Registered Office: E-4, Vaibhav Nagar, Near Tapovan Mandir, Pimpri, Pune - 411017.

2. Post Box No. 36, Pimpri Colony Post Office, Pimpri, Pune - 411017

Phone No: (+91) 9011013210 / 9146285129

You can also order your copy at the online store:
www.gethappythoughts.org

*Free Shipping plus 10% Discount on purchases above Rs. 500/-

For further details contact:
TEJGYAN GLOBAL FOUNDATION
Registered Office:

Happy Thoughts Building, Vikrant Complex,
Near Tapovan Mandir, Pimpri, Pune 411017, Maharashtra, India.
Contact No.: 020-27411240, 27412576
Email: mail@tejgyan.com

MaNaN Ashram:

Survey No. 43, Sanas Nagar, Nandoshi gaon, Kirkatwadi Phata, Sinhagad Road, Pune 411024, Maharashtra, India.

Contact No.: 992100 8060.

Hyderabad: 9885558100, **Bangalore:** 9880412588,
Delhi : 9891059875, **Nashik:** 9326967980, **Mumbai:** 9373440985

For accessing our unique 'System for Wisdom'
from self-help to self-realization, please follow us on:

	Website	www.tejgyan.org
	Online Shopping/	www.gethappythoughts.org
	Blog	
	Video Channel	www.youtube.com/tejgyan For Q&A videos: http://goo.gl/YA81DQ
	Social networking	www.facebook.com/tejgyan
	Social networking	www.twitter.com/sirshree
	Internet Radio	http://www.tejgyan.org/internetradio.aspx

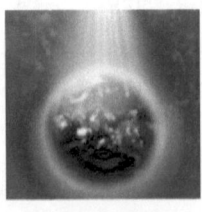

Pray for World Peace along with thousands of others every day at 09:09 am and 09:09 pm:

Divine White Light of Love, Bliss, and Peace is showering
The Golden Light of Higher Consciousness is rising
Every negativity on Earth is dissolving
Everyone is healthy, happy, and peacefully evolving
Dear God, thank you for each and every blessing.

www.ingramcontent.com/pod-product-compliance
Lightning Source LLC
LaVergne TN
LVHW041712070526
838199LV00045B/1319